THE
PITCHFORK
REVIEW

RIDE THE BUS

The Festi-val Issue

ILLUSTRATION BY STEFHANY YEPES LOZANO

"One true and deep characteristic of festivals, going back at least to Woodstock, was a guaranteed escape."

JESSE JARNOW

CONTRIBUTORS

Gabriel Alcala — Julian Baker — Matteo Berton

Noelle Bullion — Jace Clayton — Grayson Haver Currin

Anya Davidson — Michael DeForge — Camille Dodero

Ryan Dombal — Kate Fernandez — Andrew Gaerig

Stevie Gee — David Brandon Geeting — Michael A. Gonzales

Ron Hart — William Hartman — Lucy Hewett

Marc Hogan — Jesse Jarnow — Matthew Johnson

Evan Luchessi Leon — Stefhany Yepes Lozano — Jillian Mapes

Daniel Martin-McCormick — Michaelangelo Matos

Jazz Monroe — Quinn Moreland — Jesse Nield — Tommi Parrish

Ramy — Michael Renaud — Mark Richardson

Shelby Rodeffer — Matthew Schnipper — Alex Schubert

Hyde Segal — Philip Sherburne — Laura Snapes — Sam Sodomsky

Anna Spysz — Jacob Stead — Bill Stites — Brandon Stosuy

Jessica Viscius — Crawfie Ward — Shawn Webb — Cei Willis

ALL IN THE FAMILY

STEVIE GEE

Stevie Gee (*steviegee.com*) drew the rad illustrations for our bus, but we almost gave the gig to his children. Rosa taught us know how to be a cool kid (tips in the illustration below) and Jesse nailed the wide spectrum of musicians and fans.

ROSA MARIA GEE

JESSE LEONARD GEE

Big big thanks also to **Kate Fernandez** & **Shawn Webb** for lovely modeling & impromptu dancing; **Denise Reed-Burbon** & the **Chicago Park District**, **Gina Doctor** & **MNML**, **TJ Annerino** & **Goose Island**, & **Ben Foch** for letting us bus up their spaces.

PHISH DINNER

Jesse Jarnow

"If you could engineer the perfect band for punks to make fun of, you'd probably come up with something like Phish," says Jesse Jarnow, WFMU DJ, and author of the recently published *Heads: A Biography of Psychedelic America*. For years, he has explored the relationships between artists and audiences in underground scenes, from early indie culture (*Big Day Coming: Yo La Tengo and the Rise of Indie Rock*) to modern jam bands and festivals. His story in this issue discusses what makes this particular jam band and their legendary festivals a symbol for the inherent, unstoppable power of music.

In all his work, Jarnow conveys his deep research with a poetic lyricality and an insider's passion for the music. "There are very few acts that play like Phish, that have spent as much time devoted to close listening exercises or playing charted and composed music. The amount of work required to become Phish is staggering," says Jarnow, discussing his deep and long-standing appreciation for the group. "That Phish can draw tens of thousands of people to watch them improvise is still pretty magical," he muses, "And, I think, will remain so."

BEEP BEEP! BUS RIDES

Shelby Rodeffer & Julian Baker
Painted the bus with flying colors. Literally. Both are accomplished illustrators and designers to boot. Check them out: *shelbyrodeffer.com* and *juliansbaker.com*

Crawfie Ward
Drove the 1979 Prevost Bus from Indiana to Chicago, manuevered it around the city for our photo shoot (and then some). Can't get mad.

Lucy Hewett
Shot the bus and made it beautiful. Thanks to her and her crack team (William Hartman & Jesse Nield), the cover photograph happened. *lucyhewett.com*

ILLUSTRATION BY STEVIE GEE

The Pitchfork Review is a registered trademark of Advance Magazine Publishers Inc. Copyright © 2016 Condé Nast. All Rights Reserved. Printed in the U.S.A.

The Pitchfork Review No. 10, Summer 2016 (ISBN 978-0-9975626-0-6) is published four times per year by Condé Nast, which is a division of Advance Magazine Publishers Inc. The Pitchfork Review Principal Office: 3317 W. Fullerton Ave., Chicago, IL 60647.

Condé Nast Principal Office: One World Trade Center, New York, NY 10007. S. I. Newhouse, Jr., Chairman Emeritus; Charles H. Townsend, Chairman; Robert A. Sauerberg, Jr., Chief Executive Officer and President; David E. Geithner, Chief Financial Officer; Jill Bright, Chief Administrative Officer.

Subscription rate in the U.S. for 4 issues is $49.99. Address all editorial, business, and production correspondence to Ryan Kennedy at ryank@pitchfork.com. Address all advertising inquiries to ads@pitchfork.com. For permissions and reprint requests, please contact info@thepitchforkreview.com. The Pitchfork Review is distributed by Publishers Group West and printed by Palmer Printing Inc., 739 S. Clark St., Chicago, IL 60605. Visit us online at thepitchforkreview.com. To subscribe to Condé Nast magazines on the World Wide Web, visit condenastdigital.com. Set in typefaces from Alias (alias.dj), Grilli Type (grillitype.com), and Klim Type Foundry (klim.co.nz). Printed on Mohawk Via and Endurance Cover Silk from Veritiv.

The Pitchfork Review does not read or accept unsolicited submissions and is not responsible for the return or loss of, or damage to unsolicited manuscripts, unsolicited artwork (including, but not limited to, drawings, photographs, and transparencies), or any other unsolicited materials.

Illustration by Stevie Gee.

Ryan Schreiber
Editor-in-Chief/Founder
Chris Kaskie
President
Michael Renaud
Vice President & Creative Director

Editorial

Mark Richardson
Executive Editor
Matthew Schnipper
Managing Editor
Amy Phillips
News Director
Ryan Dombal
Senior Editor
Jayson Greene
Senior Editor
Jillian Mapes
Senior Editor
Jeremy Gordon
Deputy News Editor
Jenn Pelly
Associate Editor
Evan Minsker
Associate Editor, News
Stacey Anderson
Associate Features Editor
Philip Sherburne
Contributing Editor
Laura Snapes
Contributing Editor
Marc Hogan
Senior Staff Writer
Kevin Lozano
Staff Writer
Matthew Strauss
Staff Writer
Quinn Moreland
Assistant Editor
Jazz Monroe
Associate Staff Writer
Sheldon Pearce
Associate Staff Writer

Noah Yoo
Associate Staff Writer
Sam Sodomsky
Editorial Fellow
Alex Newhouse
Editorial Fellow
Corey Smith-West
Editorial Fellow

Advertising

Zachary Davis
Head of Revenue
Matt Frampton
Vice President, Sales
Adam Krefman
Director, Sales & Business Development
Rob Jensen
Senior Account Manager
Jared Heiman
Director, Sales
Seth Dodson
Integrated Marketing Manager
Emily Curtis
Media Planner

Operations

John Jung
Vice President of Strategy & Operations
Ryan Kennedy
Director of Finance & Operations
Charlotte Zoller
Director of Social Media
Stephanie Downes
Director of Audience Development
Courtney Cox
Office Manager, Brooklyn
Amelia Dobmeyer
Internal Communications Manager

Product

Matt Dennewitz
Vice President, Product
Neil Wargo
Senior Developer
Mark Beasley
Creative Technologist
Andrew Gaerig
Developer, Analyst

Design

Joy Burke
Digital Art Director
Noelle Bullion
Art Director
Jessica Viscius
Senior Graphic Designer
Nicole Ginelli
Interactive Designer
Jojo Sounthone
Graphic Design Fellow

Video

RJ Bentler
Vice President, Video Programming
Ash Slater
Producer
Michael Garber
Director
Jim Larson
Director
Jon Leone
Director
Rio Mineta
Editor
Anthony Esquivel
Motion Designer
Matt Caldamone
Motion Designer
Garrett Weinholtz
Channel Manager

This issue's editor was **Matthew Schnipper,** who worked alongside **Mark Richardson, Camille Dodero, Ryan Dombal, Jillian Mapes,** and **Quinn Moreland.** It was designed and art directed by **Noelle Bullion** and **Jessica Viscius. Ryan Kennedy**, **Courtney Cox** and **Amelia Dobmeyer** looked after the operations. **Michael Renaud** drove the bus.

The New York Times Reviews Woodstock

AUGUST 18TH, 1969

For many, the weekend had been the fulfillment of months of planning and hoping, not only to see and hear the biggest group of pop performers ever assembled, but also to capture the excitement of camping out with strangers, experimenting with drugs and sharing—as one youth put it— "an incredible unification."

—— Barnard L. Collier

The Reign of the Giant Hamster Ball

By Quinn Moreland

Just to be clear, the gigantic hamster balls that have become main stage music-festival spectacles are water balls—or "water walking balls," according to the sellers hawking the recreational toys for up to $325 on eBay. They are not the balls used for Zorbing (aka globe riding), a thrill-seeking New Zealand pastime in which one climbs into a double layer of spherical plastic and catapults down hills. Water balls, rather, are intended to make sport of walking on water and, in less divine moments, they're used to surf on the heads and hands of dehydrated, molly-crazed audiences.

Wayne Coyne of the Flaming Lips is the most infamous perpetrator of these balls, seemingly taking every opportunity possible to parade atop the bodies that fill festivals to see his band. At any given point during the psychedelic kaleidoscope that is a Flaming Lips set, Coyne slips offstage, where a team helps him through a zippered entrance into the deflated sack, which is then sealed and inflated. The Boy in the Bubble born anew, Coyne carefully trots back to the stage's edge and rolls onto the crowd. If you have ever witnessed a pet rodent wobble around in a hard plastic orb, you will know that it is not the most graceful activity. The same goes for humans:

Few people are able to surf smoothly across heads and hands. Instead, they fall and crawl, repeatedly, like an infant learning how to walk. Although he is among the most experienced human hamsters, Coyne is usually quick to stumble to his knees as hands clamber to touch him, only to be obstructed by an impenetrable plastic wall that separates performer and audience. Another notorious crowd walker is Diplo, who sometimes rolls around in the orb during Major Lazer performances. Both musicians typically perform the stunt in button-ups and slacks, giving an odd sense of professionalism to the job of being a human bowling ball.

But while the hamster ball has been all fun and games for Coyne and Diplo, it has strangely been the cause of controversy for others. In 2014, Akon performed inside a bubble at a Democratic Republic of the Congo concert celebrating the United Nations' International Day of Peace. Unfortunately for the Senegalese-American rapper, Africa was in the midst of a horrific Ebola crisis and fans thought he'd donned the silly space bubble as an isolation chamber from the virus.

This rumor turned out to be false. However, the scandal raises a good point: Inflatable hamster balls are very imposing, and even when those inside the bubble mean well, they inevitably squish all that's in their path. The best thing anyone can do is stay out of the way. ✐

QUINN MORELAND *is assistant editor at* Pitchfork.

Illustrations by Gabriel Alcala

Top Six Festival Headline Sets of Our Dreams

Kate Bush performs on an actual cloud

Jay Z does *The Blueprint* in full with no other songs and doesn't talk at all

Animal Collective and the Grateful Dead (no Bob Weir songs)

Jamie xx plays jungle for 12 straight hours

Metallica performs only songs written before 1990

Frank Ocean (please)

The Last Band at Bonnaroo

By Grayson Haver Currin

One might assume that Ashley Capps has run out of memory for more bands.

For the last 15 summers, Capps has thrown a party—sometimes for as many as 100,000 people and sometimes with more than 100 bands—on an enormous farm an hour southeast of Nashville. That would be Bonnaroo, one of many projects from Capps' long-running, Knoxville-based empire AC Entertainment and one of America's most mammoth festivals. Since its 2002 inception, Bonnaroo has perennially put the biggest musicians in the world, from Billy Joel and Elton John to Kanye West and James Brown, onstage just after the blistering Tennessee sun has set. Somehow, though, Capps not only remembers the last name on 2006's 118-band roster, capped by Tom Petty and Radiohead, but also that very act's set. That year's performance by the then relatively unknown Zac Brown Band lingers with Capps. "It was one of those shows where you realize you're watching someone who's on the cusp of really connecting with a larger audience," remembers Capps. Watching the Atlanta-based Brown, he expected the group would soon be famous, just as his friends from Georgia had told him. "There was clearly this connection, and there's an energy with that where you can feel it."

He was right: Only two years later, Brown would release his triple-platinum breakthrough *The Foundation* and become a strange modern-country superstar, known as much for his omnipresent and meticulously groomed beard as for his willingness to push his roots-rock act into unexpected realms. Before

that, though, he was an early member of an ongoing, entirely circumstantial fraternity of motley musical acts when he stepped onstage in Manchester, Tennessee—that is, the fraternity of the last bands listed on the Bonnaroo poster.

Determining the last act on the Bonnaroo poster each year isn't exactly a direct process. Between the initial lineup announcement and the moment when bands arrive on the grounds in early June, the roster—and with it, the poster—can shift through many iterations. As the festival has worked to stay unpredictable with movie events (Lebowski Fest in 2009, for instance) or cadres of comedians (in 2005, eight comics were

tacked onto the end of the bill like forgotten punchlines), the last lines can get messy. The festival maintains a detailed online repository of its bookings, though, each meant to serve as the year's final poster.

"You look at some of the artists in that group, like Zac," Capps says with a chuckle, "and you say, 'Well, maybe I want to be last, too.'"

Indeed, though Brown may be the most famous person in that list of 15, he's certainly not its only success. Strangely, Toots & the Maytals were

the last band on the 2003 Bonnaroo poster, after having served as reggae icons for four decades. Warpaint became the ninth official afterthought in 2010, months before the four-piece released its Rough Trade debut. Among the other acts with this peculiar distinction, there's erstwhile old-time standouts the Biscuit Burners and mash-up progenitor Z-Trip, affable Malaysian singer Zee Avi and peripatetic troubadour Willy Mason.

But there are a few acts for which a Bonnaroo postscript remains a pinnacle, the crown on what may have, at that point, seemed like promising careers. British alt-rock group Your Vegas played in 2008, two months after releasing its one major-label album and two years before breaking up altogether. Though former frontman Coyle Girelli seemed eager to be interviewed, being the last band at Bonnaroo wasn't a topic he wanted to entertain (upon learning about this piece's focus, he soon stopped responding altogether).

Likewise, the New York electronic-pop duo Tiny Victories held that final slot in 2012 and are now on hiatus. Singer Greg Walters, however, talks about his Bonnaroo experience with great enthusiasm and detail. Months earlier, Tiny Victories released its first EP and were surprised by the amount of attention its emphatic, colorful little tunes earned. And then, days before Bonnaroo began, an email arrived asking the band to make the half-day drive to Tennessee for a last-minute, late-night set on a tiny stage for those fans who weren't ready to go to bed after the headliners were finished. As 80,000 people dispersed, Tiny Victories would give them one more chance to revel.

17

Illustrations by Gabriel Alcala

"We started setting up in the middle of the night, in the middle of the main square, where all these people would walk past to go back to their campgrounds," Walters remembers. "We were the last band on the bill, but goddammit, we had one of the best slots."

Just before Tiny Victories were about to play, however, rain began to fall. The ad hoc stage included a lot of high-end electronics but no basic cover overhead. "It was the only stage at Bonnaroo that was not ready for bad weather. They had a great sound system, but they did not have a tarp. And we're an electronica band, so we can't just unplug," Walters says. And so, Tiny Victories took the loss. "We had barreled down to get there and taken time off from our jobs for this one show," he recalls. "But we got back in the van and drove back to New York City."

Because Tiny Victories hadn't actually performed at Bonnaroo, organizers asked them to return next year. They accepted and advanced four slots to the right on the 2013 poster, where they led the final line rather than closed it. That distinction went, instead, to Nashville guitarist William Tyler.

"I wasn't aware that was my spot," Tyler says now. "This makes me wonder if it's better to be the last four lines in the NCAA Tournament or the first four in the NIT."

Still, the opportunity had a profound impact on Tyler's musical trajectory. When Bonnaroo reached out to Tyler's booking agent, festival organizers asked if his full band could play. To date, though, the longtime Lambchop sideman had only issued three albums of *solo* guitar instrumentals. He had no band, but the offer sounded like a welcome challenge. For Nashville musicians, playing the massive festival to the east seemed like a necessary rite of passage.

Tyler quickly assembled an electric quartet and reimagined many of the quiet songs of his past. His next EP, *Lost Colony*, featured that same crew and set the stage for the ambitious *Modern Country*, his first full-length effort with a full band, anchored by Wilco drummer Glenn Kotche.

"That Bonnaroo experience made me realize, 'OK, you can play instrumental music and connect with people who wouldn't necessarily be into it, if it's loud and it moves—like a jam band, basically,'" he says. "That was my first experience thinking of my music outside of insular, experimental, private folk music. I realized, 'Oh, yeah, we can sound like the Allman Brothers if we want to.' And that's led to so many other things."

Four years after Zac Brown ranked last on the Bonnaroo roster, the frontman returned to the festival. With Hot 100 hits now in tow, Brown had climbed from the bottom rung to the seventh of more than three-dozen rows of artists, displayed just beneath LCD Soundsystem and The National but far above the likes of the xx, the Crystal Method, and clear stylistic forebearer, Kris Kristofferson.

For Capps, watching such an ascent remains one of the thrills of his lifelong business.

"It's always fascinating to see how it all turns out," he says. "There are a lot of great instances where a band that's an 'opening act' steals the show. It's a very unscientific process," Capps admits. This year, Zack Heckendorf, a songwriter who seems descended from former Bonnaroo co-headliner Dave Matthews, will take those last-slot honors. "There are always moments where the hierarchy gets reversed later on, and I still find that really exciting." ✎

GRAYSON HAVER CURRIN *lives in Raleigh, North Carolina. He has written for Pitchfork since 2006 and is the music editor of INDY Week.*

Best Places to Nap at a Festival

1. Silent disco tent
2. Backseat of random new Toyota that is always on display
3. Broken Porta Potty
4. Standing in crowd during 40-minute Kanye rant
5. Curled up inside Deadmau5' helmet

FESTIVAL JOKES

What kind of computer does today's most popular British singer use? A Dell

What kind of band gets you sweet and sticky? A jam band

Why is the eastside the worst place to watch your favorite rapper? Because Kanye West

HIGH LIFE

The Champagne of Beers

EVERY BUBBLE, A TINY AMBASSADOR OF QUALITY.

miller ®

HIGH LIFE ®

The Champagne of Beers

Drums! Drums! All Drums!

He eats cymbals, wears a chain collar, and swallows
Insta-Grow Pills by the jar. With a major U.S.
festival appearance on the way, famed Muppet
percussionist Animal speaks: "Rock'n'roll!!!!!!!!!"

Interview by Quinn Moreland

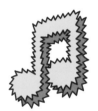

Forget about the LCD Soundsystem reunion, Radiohead mystery concerts, and those Dead & Company resurrections. This summer's most exciting music festival appearance comes courtesy of a much more recognizable ensemble: Dr. Teeth and the Electric Mayhem, the Muppets house band, will perform at San Francisco's Outside Lands in August. Since an IRL appearance by the psych-rock five-piece is rare, *The Pitchfork Review* chatted over email with legendary drummer-barbarian Animal and mellow bassist Sgt. Floyd Pepper, who assisted with translations, interpretations, and interventions.

TPR **What most excites you about Outside Lands?**

ANIMAL   Rock 'n' roll! Rock 'n' roll!!!!!!!!!

SGT. FLOYD PEPPER   Animal is an aficionado of the righteous music that's gonna be happening at Outside Lands. He loves gettin' his groove on, hangin' with the other bands, and doin' whatever it is that drummers do when they get together. A very strange tribe, those drummers. As for me, I'm lookin' forward to the beer.

What are your music festival necessities?

ANIMAL   Drums! Big drums. That all.

SGT. F. P.   It's all about the basics with Animal. Bring the drums and he's good to go. Fact is, even if he forgets his drums, I'm sure he'll find something to create the proper percussive vibe. Just don't stand too close when he does. My only demand at a music festival is good vibes, a working mojo... and beer.

In a promo vido for Outside Lands, which stars the Electric Mayhem, Animal is very excited that Radiohead is also playing the festival. Animal, what do you like about Radiohead?

ANIMAL   Radiohead! Radiohead! LOUD!!!!!!!!!!!!

SGT. F. P.   Loud—that's Animal's highest praise. He appreciates the volume of their creativity and the creativity of

their volume. Plus, last time we saw Radiohead, they let Animal ride with their roadies. Radiohead roadies rock.

If you were given the chance to book Woodstock 2016, who would you want on the bill?

ANIMAL   Drums! Drums! All drums! Dave Grohl! Andy Hurley! Phil Selway! Matt Helders! Michael Miley! Shannon Larkin! Tommy Clufetos! Questlove! Brent Fitz! Sheila E.! More! More!

SGT. F. P.   You asked for it, friend. It's gonna be an all-percussion orchestra. Anyone in attendance is advised to bring a backup set of eardrums.

Animal, you recently faced Dave Grohl and Fall Out Boy's Andy Hurley in televised drum battles. Who is your next opponent?

ANIMAL   Grohl! Hurley! Animal win!

SGT. F. P.   Yeah, Animal recently went mano-a-drummo with Dave Grohl [on an episode of "The Muppets"] and Andy Hurley of Fall Out Boy [at the Radio Disney Music Awards]. He's convinced he whupped 'em, but they're still reviewing the wreckage before they announce a winner. As for who's next, that depends on whether we can score some low-cost drum replacement insurance.

Do you still eat your drumsticks?

ANIMAL   Wood, yes. Chicken, no.

SGT. F. P.   He's vegan when it comes to drumsticks.

You two have been in a band together since 1975. What does it mean to be a rock star in 2016?

ANIMAL   Break things! Women! Get paid!

SGT. F. P.   Yeah, it's pretty much the same as it ever was. But with more artisanal beers.

Animal, will you ever release a solo record?

ANIMAL   Come soon. Can't miss.

SGT. F. P.   Animal's been working on a solo record for as long as I've known him. It's a concept album: *Songs in the Key of Loud.* Download it with care.

ANIMAL   Outside Lands! Rock 'n' roll!

SGT. F. P.   Dig you later. ✐

QUINN MORELAND *is assistant editor at Pitchfork.*

21

Wedding Bells at a Headbanger's Ball: Ozzfest's Unholy Matrimony VIP Package By Marc Hogan

On August 14, 2004, the Wisconsin village of East Troy was a beautiful place to get married. The sky over the Alpine Valley Music Theatre, an outdoor amphitheater nestled among lush hills, was clear and blue. The temperature peaked, records show, around a pleasant 72 degrees Fahrenheit. For David Dennis and Kerri Howard of Rockford, Ill., the massive, 37,000-capacity venue

held another attraction that day: Ozzfest, the annual touring music festival devoted to hard rock and heavy metal, during which the happy couple took the stage to say "I do" right after a characteristically aggressive set by horror-masked Iowa band Slipknot.

Marriage proposals aren't rare at concerts, metal shows not except-

ed, but weddings are another matter. The Dennises were something of an anomaly, securing their public ceremony through a loose connection to an employee at events giant Clear Channel (since renamed Live Nation). But the two, who met cutting hair at Pegasus Hair Styling—David's business back in Rockford—weren't the only ones interested in tying the knot at Ozzy and Sharon Osbourne's traveling hesher circus. In 2010, six years after David and Kerri became man and wife there, Ozzfest started offering the "Unholy Matrimony VIP Package." The $266-per-person price included 10 pit tickets (for the bride and groom, plus an eight-person wedding party), a champagne toast, a cake, and a backstage tour led by Ozzy's stage assistant, "Big" Dave Moscato—who'd also gotten ordained to officiate the nuptials.

Moscato, calling from Black Sabbath's recent Australian tour, tells me he only remembers doing "about three or four" weddings during Ozzfest's 2010 installment, which was an abbreviated six dates. Still, he describes the decision to offer a VIP wedding package—reached within the 60 seconds it took him to sign up online and become a reverend—as a response to an occasional demand that'd emerged since the festival's 1996 beginning. "Metalheads are a different breed," he says. "They are such huge fans, and that's one way you could be a part of it." It didn't hurt, he reasons, that an Ozzfest wedding allowed an escape from parents and other meddlesome loved ones who might interfere with how the event should be run.

David and Kerri were engaged in 2004, but hadn't set a date. Kerri had a customer at the salon whose daughter lived in the Los Angeles area, and the daughter's roommate worked for Clear Channel. Ozzfest was coming soon, and Kerri was a huge Ozzy fan. "I kind of joked and said, 'Let's get married in the parking lot at Ozzfest,'" David remembers. "Kerri's customer called her daughter, her daughter talks to her roommate, and her roommate says, 'I can get you married onstage.'" Dave was a widower, and a nephew of his first wife—who'd died from cancer—conducted the ceremony. They didn't meet Ozzy, and David describes throngs of sweaty, predominantly male Slipknot fans screaming at Kerri, who's "a good-looking girl," to "take it off." Trojan had a booth at the fest, so the newlyweds were also showered with condoms. All in all, though, he says, "It was a good time." The two held a separate ceremony about a month later at his farm south of Rockford, and they're still married to this day.

Laura Russum and Joshuah Bogus of Dover, Delaware—who were hitched at the 2010 Ozzfest stop in Camden, New Jersey—had a different experience. "It was the worst rain of the entire tour," Ozzy's assistant Moscato says. Laura says her husband—they, too, have remained together—is a music lover, and when traditional matrimonial planning wasn't getting them very far, they decided to have a backyard ceremony for family and friends and an Ozzfest wedding just for fun: "Who doesn't want to feel like a rock star for one day?"

The Boguses were supposed to exchange vows on the outdoor stage, right before a performance by Zakk Wylde's band Black Label Society,

but they ended up inside, on the main stage, due to the storm. The weather wasn't the only disappointment: Getting a marriage license in

Kerri & David Dennis exchange vows and pose with Slipknot

New Jersey was a hassle, they didn't meet anyone famous, and they spent all day waiting around in the not-so-exciting VIP area; plus, Joshuah volunteered his time playing guitar in a church band that kicked him out when the choir leader and priest learned he'd be trading rings amid devil's horns. (The bride and groom didn't even attend the church.)

Not surprisingly, Laura doesn't recommend the overall experience. But she does advocate that other engaged couples do what they want and not worry about everyone else. "I still love our backyard wedding the most," she admits, "but the Ozzfest wedding makes for a good story." ✐

MARC HOGAN *is based in Iowa and is a senior staff writer at Pitchfork.*

Illustrations by Gabriel Alcala

What's the over/under on your favorite band gracing festival stages next summer? Pitchfork's oddsmakers break it down.

The Smiths Odds: Poor
You know Coachella has to try this every year, and if they can't throw enough vegan promises at Morrissey to make this happen, no one can.

Operation Ivy Odds: Decent
Ska will never go away.

Sonic Youth Odds: Abysmal
For Sonic Youth to reunite would mean for Thurston Moore and Kim Gordon to un-divorce after he cheated on her. You'll likely have to get your guitar squall elsewhere. Thanks a lot, Thurston.

Destiny's Child Odds: Low
Beyoncé is too busy ruling the world to give Kelly and Michelle any table scraps.

Talking Heads Odds: Good
David Byrne's fancy bikes and expensive white suits don't pay for themselves.

R.E.M. Odds: Not great
Michael Stipe is too busy growing his ginormous beard.

Chuck Hughes Makes the Best Festival Food on Earth

By Quinn Moreland

Arcade Fire enjoyed the fried Mars bars. Jessie Ware loved the oysters. Portugal. The Man even volunteered in the kitchen. That's how well-regarded the food is backstage at Montreal's annual Osheaga Music and Arts Festival. For the last seven years, the Québécois fest has invited chef and Food Network personality Chuck Hughes—co-owner of locally renowned restaurants Le Bremner and Garde Manger—to cater the artist area. "We've given ourselves the mandate to blow everybody's mind," says Hughes, a onetime "Iron Chef America" contestant whose elaborate backstage spread includes 20-foot meat smokers, jerk crab, pizza ovens, smoothie stations, and lemon meringue pie. Hughes and his team—a crew of about 50 who work the festival line—take their job very seriously, compiling ideas all year long. "It's not just about serving food," says the chef. "It's about giving an experience."

TPR **How did you become involved with Osheaga?**

CH When I was 18, 19, 20, I was a roadie. I loved the music scene but wasn't a musician, so I started my own little catering company for bands. I'd go on tours and cook backstage; I used to do catering at Warped Tour. Then life happened: I went to cooking school, started cooking in restaurants, opened my own place. When this opportunity came, it brought me back to the time when I didn't have two restaurants, kids, responsibilities—when my job was to go out there, cook, and have a good time.

What's a day for you like at Osheaga?

At festivals, you're going to war pretty much every day. That's the mentality: You never know what's going to happen. A day starts at 5:45 a.m. There's nobody there, just me and a of couple guys. Breakfast starts at 8 a.m. and it's load-in, so you have truckers, techies, and some musicians—if they're still up. From then on, it doesn't stop all day. I always define my job there as lighting fires and putting out fires: running around to get everything organized, making sure tour managers are happy, and the food's the best that it can possibly be. We shut down at around 10 o'clock at night. Then it's a general clean up and a mad dash to catch the last band.

Your Osheaga menu is more complex than traditional festival fare. What foods have you featured over the years?

We do food that's elevated, but not fancy. Just really good. I have everything—gluten-free, vegan—and if I don't, I'll make it on the spot. We have grills, hibachis, barbecues. We have our own pastry section—everything from croissants, buns, and breads to Jell-O shots, puddings, cakes. We have a shake station and a deli. We have Italian: a mozzarella bar, a pasta bar, salads, all kinds of roasted vegetables, olives. A soft-serve ice cream and coffee bar. A taco station. A paella station. A raw bar. We do jerk crab and that's become a festival classic. People love it. When you have your favorite band walking through and saying, "Guys, the food's amazing!" there's nothing more rewarding. ✐

QUINN MORELAND *is assistant editor at* Pitchfork.

Illustrations by Gabriel Alcala

25

~~~~~~

Chuck Hughes' Jerk Crab   Prep: 10 min   Cook: 5 min   Serves: 4

INGREDIENTS

1/4 CUP (60 ML) WATER

1/4 CUP (60 ML) BUTTER

1 SHALLOT, FINELY CHOPPED

4 SPRIGS ROSEMARY

10 SLICES FRESH GINGER

20 CRAB LEGS (ABOUT 6 HANDFULS OR CRACKED SECTIONS)

1 TBSP (15 ML) JERK SEASONING

4 LIMES, CUT IN HALF

1/4 CUP (60 ML) CHOPPED PARSLEY LEAVES

2 TBSP (30 ML) CHOPPED CELERY LEAVES

SALT AND FRESHLY GROUND PEPPER

1. Preheat the oven to 450°F (230°C).

2. In a large ovenproof skillet, bring the water and butter to a boil. Add the shallot, rosemary, and ginger. Then add the crab legs and jerk seasoning.

3. Squeeze in the juice from two limes. Add the lime halves to the pan. Stir until the crab is thoroughly coated with the spices and the cooking liquid.

4. Put the pan in the oven for two-three minutes or until the crab is warm and infused with the herbs and spices.

Stir in the parsley and celery leaves and season with salt and pepper. Garnish with the remaining lime halves.

Note: At the restaurant, we use snow crab from Havre-Saint-Pierre. Snow crab is small and sweet. Alaskan crab legs are larger, have more meat, and are saltier. Both are very good. It's a matter of taste.

A Pitchfork Review City Guide   By Andrew Gaerig

A Short List of Things You Can Do in Chicago When Not at The Pitchfork Music Festival

Illustrations by Gabriel Alcala

U nusual both for Pitchfork and for a city guide, this list makes no effort to register the best of anything. There are plenty of such lists, and the problem isn't that they're insufficient or duplicative—though they are both—the problem is that they tend to recommend establishments that are so popular they require significant planning or gross wait times. Even if you plan ahead, those lists are not geared to the festivalgoer, whose visit to a city is often brief and mostly filled up with sweating and watching bands. Consider this a recommendation for the one or two Windy City things you must do while not singing along to Jeremih.

Look at Some Buildings

In general, avoid any temptation to hang out downtown: It's where Chicago works, but not where it lives and plays, and the area is overrun with tourists any time folks aren't working. You're going to want to stare at the pretty buildings though, so consider an architectural boat tour on the Chicago River, chill and educational in equal measure. Down there in Millennium Park, you'll find Cloud Gate, aka The Bean—the, um, bean-shaped reflective sculpture that captures the city's skyline—which is both terrifically dumb and a satisfying way to gaze at buildings and selfie sticks.

Achieve the Proper Amount of Culture

You can play Ferris Bueller at the Art Institute of Chica-go, an amazing but intimidatingly large collection. If you want to keep your Art Institute visit short, head directly to the Thorne Miniature Rooms, where you can imagine how really tiny people lived in different eras. A mile north, just off the chain-store-heavy stretch of Michigan Avenue known as the Magnificent Mile, the Museum of Contemporary Art is a more manageable alternative where you don't leave feeling guilty for not having sufficiently appreciated *A Sunday on La Grande Jatte*. Plus, it has a better gift shop.

Drink Beer with Dogs

Chicago is a neighborhood town. Go find a neighbor-hood, then find a bar in it, preferably one with a beer garden: Cody's Public House (Lakeview), Small Bar (Logan Square), and Happy Village (Wicker Park) are appealing places to drink outside near people with dogs. While in town, do try Jeppson's Malört, a Swedish liqueur available only in Chicago, taken as a shot because the flavor of bug spray is difficult to pair. You will regret this, but the cred-to-regret ratio is strongly in your favor.

Survive Stroller Derby

Speaking of neighborhoods, Wicker Park is not just an unwatched Josh Hartnett vehicle. Once the much grittier stomping grounds of musicians like Liz Phair and Tortoise, the northwestern community is now considerably more stroller friendly—you could fight a land war in Rus-

27

sia with the double-wide monstrosities—but still the finest concentration of shops, bars, and restaurants the city offers. Try Penelope's for festival-ready wares, Saint Alfred for T-shirts and sneakers Pharrell might own, or Belmont Army for the disappearing line between streetwear and army/navy surplus. Quimby's is your underground literature hub of choice and the city's best magazine selection, with a special focus on LGBT publications. Skip the fancy taco shops and head to La Pasadita.

Walk Pilsen

Pilsen is a slowly gentrifying South Side neighborhood that retains some of the grit and charm that has been developed out of Wicker Park. Amble along 18th Street, picking your way in and out of art galleries and taco joints. Here you'll find Chicago's densest concentration of DIY venues and art studios.

Hoard More Records

Perhaps you'd like to purchase records? Chicago can accommodate you. Skip comprehensive indie emporium Reckless Records for one of Chicago's specialist shops: Dusty Groove (Wicker Park) for soul and jazz; Gramaphone Records (Lincoln Park) for house and techno; Permanent Records (Ukrainian Village) for punk; Bric-a-Brac (Logan Square) for what's on the tin. Laurie's Planet of Sound isn't excellent at any one thing except feeling exactly how record stores used to feel in the 1990s.

Make a Bad Culinary Decision

The drenched Italian beef sandwich is a Chicago specialty, with Al's #1 Italian Beef, a 78-year-old family business that's grown into a franchise, winning the local vote by

plurality. Redhot Ranch in Lakeview has the best griddle burger in the city. Literally any place with an anthropomorphic hot dog on its sign will do. Vegetarians can head to Sultan's Market in Wicker Park for falafel. Don't let Guy Fieri ruin shitty food for you.

Indulge Your Craft Vices

Chicago-born Intelligentsia Coffee is now well known among coffee connoisseurs, but quality remains extremely high considering. Bow Truss is the finest of the many upstarts. For beer, Half Acre in Lincoln Square and Revolution in Avondale have tap rooms with special pours, though look for the smaller Pipeworks Brewing on local taps, because the world needs more beers that taste like coconut or cinnamon.

End Your Night

You'll want some place small and dark. Cole's in Logan Square and Rainbo Club in Wicker Park are fine choices for musically inclined dives. Zakopane, also in Wicker Park, features an unmagnificent red velvet curtain; Logan Square's Whirlaway Lounge has the city's most inconveniently placed couch. The Owl, a 10-minute walk away, is open late—until 4 a.m. on Fridays and 5 a.m. on Saturdays—and has a pleasing waterfall.

Wait a Really Long Time

Fine, if you must: The grub at Parson's and Fat Rice in Logan Square and Kuma's in Avondale is worth the scary wait times. Danny's, a Wicker Park bar in an old house, is usually the city's best low-key dance party if you can stomach the line. Bucktown's Map Room, a watering hole prominently mentioned in a Spoon song, has great taps. And head to Violet Hour in Wicker Park, if you like your drinks fancy and your decor geometric. ✎

29

ANDREW GAERIG *is a developer and analyst at Pitchfork, as well as a frequent writer.*

10
Innovative Festivals

[1] Unsound Festival

KRAKOW, POLAND

By Philip Sherburne
Photos by Anna Spysz

Deep in a cavelike basement in the medieval old town of Krakow, Poland, the members of a Viennese band called Fuckhead basted their singer, stripped to his underwear, in soap and feathers.

In the absence of a stage, they had set up their instruments in one corner of the room, on the same level as the audience; any line separating performer and spectator was purely notional. In that respect, it might have been any punk show of the past three decades. But this wasn't a punk show, exactly.

On guitar, drums, and laptop, the quartet banged out a digitally damaged variant of heavy metal. But the music was secondary to their antics, which amounted to a kind of cryptic, symbolically fraught performance art, complete with a confounding array of props—like a cardboard box fitted over the drummer's head and then broken open, yielding fistfuls of straw. One musician

snaked through the crowd, delicately stuffing cotton balls in listeners' ears. Toward the set's climax, two band members stood facing opposite walls, shorts slipped down their hips—between them, a yard's length of red string, its ends clenched between each man's buttocks. The group ended the show teetering in a human pyramid, mostly naked but for their skivvies, tattoos, and yellow rubber gloves. It must have all meant something, but—what?

Back in 2007, this was my introduction to Unsound Festival, and if the performance wasn't exactly typical for the event—that year I also saw techno DJs, ambient musicians, and a roundtable discussion about the underground art scene in Belarus, a Communist dictatorship—it wasn't exactly atypical, either. I've eagerly returned almost every year since then, both as a spectator and a participant, conducting panel discussions and, on a few occasions, DJing the festival's opening or closing parties. And I've learned that to attend Unsound is to be surprised, and sometimes flabbergasted: to discover not just new artists but entire strains of music; to have your understanding of the very nature of live music and club culture flipped on its ear. To come out, sometimes, spritzed in soap and feathers and strangers' sweat. Whatever the term "festival" may conjure for you—H&M flower crowns and bindis on white people; fist-bumping bros in "Sex, Drugs, and Dubstep" T-shirts—Unsound inhabits an entirely separate discursive universe.

Where mainstream fests are sprawling, grueling affairs designed to appeal, it would seem, to people who love dirt and queues but hate music and personal dignity, Unsound is sophisticated, playful, and downright delightful. It's also affordable: Last year's all-access pass was just 310 zloty (roughly $78), and covered nine days of programming, some 25 concerts in all, in addition to a number of talks, screenings, and other events. (This year, tickets jump to 385 zloty, or around $98.) Though it's an urban festival, it's walkable, with most of its events located between the picturesque historic city center, the elegantly dilapidated Jewish quarter of Kazimierz, and a handful of museums and ad hoc venues along the gentle curves of the River Vistula. And though Unsound stretches for an entire week, concerts are spread out, three or four per day, and rarely overlap—meaning that you can see everything you want and still have time to visit museums, peruse flea markets, and eat pierogi. Attendance for most events numbers several hundred; the weekend club nights spread a few thousand people, tops, across multiple rooms.

That's not just comfortable; it's also conducive to fostering a kind of community that's rare at any festival. Most patrons come for the whole week, so you see the same faces over and over, at shows and around town. During festival week, to set foot

BY JAZZ MONROE & LAURA SNAPES

² Marfa Myths Marfa, Texas

When Mid-March | **Booking Highlights** Parquet Courts, No Age, Awesome Tapes From Africa, Connan Mockasin's Wet Dream **What makes it special** Co-curated by Brooklyn-based label Mexican Summer, the three-day festival's relaxed, no-overlap schedule perfectly suits its remote location (population of Marfa: 1800). The programming's unorthodox venues encompass hangars, saloons, a Dairy Queen, and whatever else the art-intensive border town community can tailor for its niche concerts. "Seventy thousand people in a desert doesn't appeal to us," says founder Keith Abrahamsson. "We rely on the magic of Far West Texas to deliver the excitement." | **What happened this year** Dungen live-scored the animated classic *The Adventures of Prince Achmed* in a tiny movie theater, William Basinski played an army hangar, and Dead Moon's Fred and Toody headlined a cowboy bar.

³ Tallinn Music Week Tallinn, Estonia

When late March-early April | **Booking Highlights** Maarja Nuut, Avarus Ensemble, Shitney, Faun Racket | **What makes it special** Since Estonia regained independence in 1991, its capital has emerged as Eastern Europe's least likely cultural hub. TMW is an ideal way to explore the emerging city, not least for the festival's daring lineups, which are jammed full of local art savants, provocateurs, and anarchic oddballs. Other perks range from eccentric venues—Soviet factories, clubs with slippers-only door policies—to an annual opening speech from the Estonian president, Toomas Hendrik Ilves, a man more likely to namedrop the Velvet Underground than Václav Havel. | **What happened this year** Kultuurikatel, the factory where Andrei Tarkovsky shot the Zone in his 1979 film *Stalker*, held a "classical disco," while Seaplane Harbour, an eerie hangar-like maritime museum, hosted Russian bass-music DJ Pixelord for a spectacular closing party. Good news: The 2017 installment is already scheduled for March 27th through April 2nd.

⁴ Red Bull Music Academy New York City, New York

When late April-late May | **Booking Highlights** Anohni, Kamasi Washington, Pharoah Sanders, Diamanda Galás | **What makes it special** Red Bull Music Academy, once a "think tank" composed of elite curators and iconic guest lecturers is now a month-long collection of events in NYC. The festival, now with many international offshoots, pushes forward-facing lineups that renounce headliners and instead conjure enchanting one-offs, like this year's "spiritual jazz" night corralling Kamasi Washington with his sonic godfathers, Pharoah Sanders and Sun Ra Arkestra. Says cofounder Many Ameri: "We get to try things that are more fragile, and not tourable, so artists know they can bring us challenging ideas. Things might happen that aren't happening anywhere else." | **What happened this year** Events included sit-downs with Spike Lee and Madlib, a beatmaker roundtable with Metro Boomin, and an intimate Diamanda Galás show in an old Harlem church.

33

Facing Page: JENNY HVAL & SUSANNA, 2014   This page, clockwise from top: DEAF CENTER AT ST. CATHERINE'S, 2011; CURRENT 93, 2015; SUN O))), 2009

35

Top: CYCLOBE, 2014 Bottom: RROSE, 2015

in Krakow's Kuchnia u Doroty, a popular home-cooking spot famous for its "house specialty" (a tombstone-sized plate of potato pancakes slathered in beef goulash and sour cream) is to be confronted with a microcosm of Unsound's public: a cheerful mixture of locals, Western Europeans, Brits, and a handful of Americans. And the fact that many artists stick around for the duration—and a growing number of them, like Tim Hecker, Dean Blunt, and Kode9, seem to come back almost every year—only adds to the familial intimacy. It might just be the most civilized music festival going.

"Unsound favors exchange over transaction," says Matt Werth of New York's RVNG label, which has sent a number of its artists—including Holly Herndon, Julia Holter, and Maxmillion Dunbar—to perform there over the years. "Even when a stage elevates a performance at Unsound, physically or emotionally, the artist never feels removed from a shared experience. But it's also not uncommon to find that artist standing next to you during the festival. Unsound creates a sense of community while consistently challenging and subverting festival conventions."

Unsound's founder is Mat Schulz, an Australian novelist who, like many Western bohemians, washed up in Eastern Europe in the 1990s and, unlike most of them, never left. Dismayed by the lack of festivals in Poland devoted to risk-taking music, especially with an electronic or experimental bent, Schulz and a fellow expat set out to fill that gap with a small underground event in 2003. The first edition, which lasted three days, proved to be an inauspicious beginning. "The second night, bouncers came onstage and stopped a concert, threw us out, and told us not to return," Schulz recalls. "The last night had eight people in the audience. It was a trial by fire. But we persisted."

Today, in addition to the Krakow flagship event held every October, Unsound encompasses regular activities in New York, Toronto, and Adelaide, Australia, as well as one-offs in places like Bishkek, Kyrgyzstan, and Batumi, Georgia. (Perhaps the fact that Unsound originated in a city on Europe's so-called periphery is one of the things that has allowed it to continually tweak assumptions

5 Moogfest Durham, North Carolina

When Mid-May | **Booking highlights** Grimes, Laurie Anderson, GZA, Sunn O))) | **What makes it special** "If hedonism exists in a bubble, Moogfest is a Möbius strip," posits CEO and creative director Adam Katz. It's a fair take on this left-field music gathering, which sidelines what Katz calls "temporary" sensual pleasures—"food, sex, drugs"—to focus on "the pursuit of limitless self-expression." To wit, the festival's dextrous lineups dance at the intersection of outsider art, progressive politics, and vanguard tech, sometimes forging unlikely unions: This year's Grimes show, for instance, involved a walk-in motion-sensing installation, while Janelle Monáe gave politically charged talks on Afrofuturism. | **What happened this year** Robert Rich played an eight-hour, overnight "sleep concert" to an audience dozing on mattresses in a hotel ballroom.

6 Sonar Barcelona, Spain

When Mid-June | **Booking highlights** Kode9, Kelela, New Order, Stormzy | **What makes it special** Sónar balances cutting-edge electronic music (Helena Hauff, Danny L Harle) with a smart populist bent (James Blake, New Order) and lands somewhere between Unsound and a multi-day rave. This year, the Brits are bringing the best of their homegrown talent with the likes of Stormzy, while Red Bull Music Academy will appear for the 12th year, and promoters We Are Europe will make a staunch case for European unity on the eve of the EU election. | **What happened this year** Barcelona's metro system finally extended to accomodate the festival's late-night outer reaches.

7 Traena Music Festival Traena, Norway

When July 7-10 | **Booking Highlights** RY X, André Bratten, Mette Henriette, C Duncan | **What makes it special** Træna, a volcanic archipelago with 24-hour sunlight at festival time, lies four hours by boat from Norway's northwest coast. The far-flung excursion features mountain treks, boat saunas, and the odd whale sighting (though they'll more likely appear on your dinner plate). It's an unrivaled spectacle: The cave stage, for instance, is a centuries-old Viking burial ground. "One important feeling is that you can't easily leave," says founder Erlend Mogård-Larsen. "You have to stick together, sleep together, dance together, and enjoy music and life." | **What happens this year** Ida Maria, a Norwegian pop singer of American spirituals, will perform in an island church before André Bratten closes the festival under the midnight sun.

37

about the relationship between "center" and "margins.")

Schulz, 46, runs the organization alongside Gosia Płysa, a journalist and former law student whose involvement started as a festival volunteer in 2005, when she was just 20. They make a good pair. Płysa, who handles many of the fest's logistical aspects, is a cool-headed navigator of Polish bureaucracy, while Schulz, who oversees programming, is wry, prone to self-doubt, and mischievous, with a secret delight in chaos. In 2015, a right-wing Polish blogger accused the festival of promoting Satanism. That set off a panicked clerical chain reaction that found Unsound suddenly unwelcome in several churches where it had long presented performances. Schulz didn't exactly relish being targeted by the Polish extreme right, but you could tell he appreciated the absurdity of the situation.

In its early years, Unsound limited itself to a handful of events scattered across the city's smaller nightclubs and basement venues, but as the festival has grown, it has woven itself even deeper into the fabric of the city. The spaces it utilizes are unique. There's the afore-mentioned St. Catherine's, where the ambient and neoclassical sounds of artists like Holter, Hecker (playing the church's pipe organ, at that), and Stars of the Lid turned vaporous in the gothic structure's high stone arches. At the opposite end of the spectrum, there's a panoply of Communist-era architecture—like Kijów Centrum, a cinema that doubles as a time machine back to the height of the Space Age, and Nowa Huta, a working class suburb whose grim environs have lent added atmosphere to concerts from Sunn O))) and Swans. The crown jewel is undoubtedly the Hotel Forum, a Brutalist structure built in the 1970s along the River Vistula and long shuttered until Unsound successfully lobbied to put on events there in 2013. Today, its carpeted main hall serves as the centerpiece of the festival's weekend club programming: With its low ceilings, blond wood detailing, and champagne-flute lighting

AND I'VE LEARNED THAT

to attend Unsound is to be surprised, and sometimes flabbergasted: to discover not just new artists but entire strains of music; to have your understanding of the very nature of live music & club culture flipped on its ear.

overhead, it gives the impression of raving on a vintage cruise ship.

Unsound goes out of its way to tug attendees gently out of their everyday contexts. Even locals would have been surprised when, last year, the Chicago jazz cornetist Rob Mazurek climbed the steps of the main square's bell tower and followed the resident bugler's traditional hourly trumpet call with a min-ute of free improvisation. And Unsound's organizers seem well aware that the experience of the festival may be even more important than the music itself. For a few years, they banned photography, in the effort to counteract social media's steady pull at the edges of patrons' attention. (Last year, they rescinded the photo ban, yet phones mostly stayed pocketed—

suggesting that, miraculously, the attempt at behavioral therapy actually worked.) And in 2015, they took the unusual step of leaving a sizable portion of the lineup unannounced; attendees wouldn't learn who some headliners were until the moment the artists took the stage.

That year, deep in an underground chamber carved out of rock, in a salt mine some 30 minutes outside Krakow, the audience was plunged into foggy near darkness and presented with melancholy bumps and rustles that sounded unmistakably like the work of Burial—an artist who, as far as anyone knows, has never, ever played live. It had to be his music; despite many imitators, no one else sounds quite like him. But was it actually the reclusive dubstep musician himself hiding under that hoodie onstage, or a proxy sent by his label? Or someone else entirely? You could feel the excitement in the room and, thanks to the surprisingly good cell phone coverage down there, by the time the set was over and we all breathed fresh air again, the news of what we'd heard below ground had already rippled across the internet. Rumors swirled for days afterward, but we never did find out the real story. In an era of instant access and the perpetual news feed, not knowing was far more rewarding than knowing ever could have been. ✐

PHILIP SHERBURNE *lives in Barcelona and is a contributing editor at Pitchfork.*

⁸ Afropunk Brooklyn, New York

When August 27-28 | **Booking highlights** Janelle Monáe, Ice Cube, Tyler, the Creator, George Clinton | **What makes it special** Since launching in 2005, the vehemently inclusive, "no-hatefulness" black arts fest has become, in the words of founders Jocelyn Cooper and Matthew Morgan, "an annual family reunion," where "the community comes together from all over the world to celebrate themselves and the culture they create." Whether it's through firebrand iconoclasts (Bad Brains and Tyler, the Creator) or beloved black icons (both Lauryn Hill and Grace Jones played in 2015), glorious insurrection runs deep at NYC's best party festival. | **What happens this year** As well as launching more festivals, including one in Paris, Afropunk will expand the Brooklyn festival's scope with more installations, performance art, and live painting. Plus, there's a supergroup jam from members of Bad Brains, Fishbone, and Living Colour.

⁹ Ill Points Miami, Florida

When October 7-9 | **Booking highlights** Earl Sweatshirt, DJ Koze, Oneohtrix Point Never, Little Simz | **What makes it special** III Points is the intimate and experimental foil to Miami dance behemoth Ultra Music Festival. Set up in the gentrifying Wynwood Arts District, the three-day event boasts music, tech, art exhibits, film screenings, and panels, along with art installations and barbecue sessions. After a disorganized first year in 2013, Ill Points has shaped up and turned into a forward-thinking electronic festival that hasn't lost sight of its local roots, and whose execution is as artsy and innovative as its lineup. | **What happens this year** Miami fixtures Otto Von Schirach, DJ Le Spam, Kazoots, and Psychic Mirrors offset LCD Soundsystem's headlining slot.

¹⁰ Iceland Airwaves Reykjavik, Iceland

When November 2-6 | **Booking Highlights** Julia Holter, Lush, Minor Victories, PJ Harvey | **What makes it special** Set among various venues and tents, Iceland Airwaves is the best way to see Reykjavik, a city full of otherworldly sights. Like expressionist church Hallgrímskirkja and stunning concert hall Harpa—an Olafur Eliasson collaboration that evokes a crystallized cliff wall—along with hidden gems like Sægreifinn, a harborside shack that serves heavenly lobster soup (plus whale kebabs). A short coach ride will get you to the blackened countryside with its geysers and the Blue Lagoon's restorative waters. Plus, as founder Grimur Atlason points out, "PJ Harvey is coming to Iceland for the first time." | **What happens this year** There will be secret shows, a Wallpoetry music-themed public-art event, and literary salon Airwords—that is, unless sci-fi author and organizer Andri Snær Magnason is elected in the current presidential race. ✐

39

Jazz Monroe is a Pitchfork associate staff writer based in London. **Laura Snapes** lives in London and is a contributing editor at Pitchfork.

How to

IMAGES BY
DAVID BRANDON
GEETING

Accept That Your Phone Will Die

(YES, EVEN IF YOU COME PREPARED WITH A BACK-UP BATTERY)

It's simply The Law of Festivals. While charging stations are common at fests, who wants to miss Kanye to wait in line just to get to 15 percent? Write down any emergency phone numbers and your must-see sets for each day, and put the pieces of paper in a small Ziploc bag, which you can use for your phone as well if it starts raining (which it will—Fest Law dictates as such).

Pack a Bag

The temptation to be free is understandable, but festivals can be a bit of a mixed bag—which is why you should always pack one. Essentials include earplugs, sunglasses, an empty water bottle (since nearly all fests have water refill stations now), sunscreen, hand sanitizer, one of those fold-up plastic ponchos that are much cheaper when it isn't already raining, tiny and adorable packs of tissues, maybe even an extra pair of socks. You won't regret the baggage when you're in a bind, and you won't be resigned to saggy cargo shorts just to lug your essentials.

Wear a Big-Ass Hat

"But hats aren't my style," you doth protest. Well, skin cancer is definitely no one's style. If you plan on being in the sun for more than 14 seconds, pop on something with a 360-degree brim—it'll protect the back of your neck and fold up easily when dusk hits. Bucket hats are, inexplicably, big with the kids these days, so at least you'll look like an on-trend dweeb.

go to a festival

Roll in Late

Festivals are a classic eyes-bigger-than-your-stomach situation. Getting there at noon for the first batch of bands and raging all the way through the afterparty can be tough to pull off without scary drugs or the energy of a teenager (or both), particularly when it's super hot and you're drinking, too. If you really care about the headliners, save your energy and show up during the late afternoon after the sun is at its peak.

Cut the Crowd—But Don't Be a Dick

Scope out the scene. How tightly packed are the bodies? Sardine level or scattered pockets of people apathetically texting? If it's the former, know that everyone will think you're a selfish asshole. Push through—mentally and physically. The key to getting up front is planning your path before entering the crowd and weaving sideways through any pockets of space instead of barging through clearly defined groups. Apologize as much as possible. It may not make anyone else feel better, but you will.

like an expert

HOW TO ORGANIZE YOUR OWN FESTIVAL

BY BRANDON STOSUY

When I was 17, I booked a music festival on my father's farm. The Indie 500 lasted two days, about 1000 people came, and the stage was a hay truck. That was a long time ago, but I still try to keep that kind of excited, nervous spirit alive in the events I organize. It's just that now I actually know what I'm doing. As an experienced old person, I book Basilica Soundscape, a two-day "anti-festival" that takes place in a 19th century factory in Hudson, New York. We limit the audience to 1400, don't have sponsors, and aim to keep the lineup small, particular, and multi-disciplinary. It's been successful so far: In the five years of Basilica, I've never spotted anyone in attendance wearing a flower crown.

In an idealistic, punk, all-inclusive sense, anyone can put on a festival. But, in reality, it takes a certain kind of person. You have to be detail-oriented, obsessive, and able to deal with major setbacks (and major personalities) without passing out. That said, if you find yoursvelf tempted by the proposition, and want to test the waters and your own mettle, it's helpful knowing where to begin. Here are some basic steps to get you started.

First off, ask yourself why you want to book a festival. There are tons of festivals, more than anyone needs. What will make yours different? Meditate on this. Think about Altamont.

If you think you can bring something unique to the festival calendar, choose an interesting place to host your event. A lot of festivals take

place with fairly boring backdrops; if you have an unique place to host things, you're already a step ahead. Still, unless you want a special smaller destination-festival, where the journey to the festival is part of the fun, make sure it's easy for the

audience to get there. I remember going to a festival on an island years ago, and most people left before the last band was halfway through (and the last band was Radiohead) because they were all afraid of waiting in line to escape.

But be adventurous! I've done shows in basements and attics and backyards. Once I booked three floors of the New Museum (Grimes played in the glass-walled Sky Room, while Trash Talk destroyed things in the basement theater). I've also done shows in record stores and garages. I once had Pharmakon play in a bookstore, Björk DJ in a parking garage, and amateur wrestlers fight before a black metal show in a warehouse. Keep in mind if you're using a space where shows don't generally happen, you're going to have to spend money

43

on a sound system and anything else a traditional venue might've supplied. You'll need staff, too, if there isn't one attached to the venue—people to handle the doors, security, bartenders, stage and production managers. The benefit to using a readymade club is that they'll have a P.A. and staff on hand. And a liquor license (oh yeah, you'll need one of those, too). The downside is that it can be kind of boring.

Björk and Brandon Stosuy (right) DJing Bushwick DIY spot Above the Auto Parts Store

Now, this is crucial: No matter where the festival ends up being, make sure you have enough toilets. When I put on that festival at my dad's farm, I only rented one Porta Potty. It filled up quickly. Major miscalculation. The event happened over the Fourth of July. I managed to find someone to drain it half-way through the weekend, and we survived, but we were very close to a fairly disgusting disaster.

Don't overbook the festival. You also don't need to book every band in a 100-yard radius. Be picky. Think of yourself as a curator, not just someone mindlessly adding all the "big"

bands in any given genre or scene. Try to connect the bands in an interesting way. Think of their histories or some overall themes. Include non-musical stuff, too, like art and literature. But stay as rigorous in those zones as you would with the music— Focus on maintaining quality across all aspects of your festival.

As you book the bands, you'll begin receiving lengthy hospitality riders. Don't panic. In festival situations, you generally don't buy everything on the rider for each and every band. It's too expensive, and when there are dozens of acts on a bill, bands don't really expect to get all of it anyway. When I was in college I booked an experimental guitarist in my friend's attic, and because I didn't know any better, I bought everything on his rider. He almost fainted when he showed up: I think I was the first person to ever fulfill it completely. I was out $350 for something that hadn't even been expected.

Of course, this can be a case-by-case thing. If you book Kanye West, make sure to get all the stuff on his rider. And other stuff pops up, too. I recently booked a show where I was repeatedly asked to get hot water for a singer with a sore throat. I kept sending someone from the venue to the coffee shop next door, but by the time he'd find the singer, the water would be "too cold." In situations like this, you can't just bash that singer on the head like you may want to do.

You have to smile, say you'll get some more water, and move on.

Pay attention to the tech riders. These are more important than the right brand of hummus. If someone needs a special hand drum or in-ear monitor, and you don't have it when they hit the stage, there will be issues. If you're not familiar with tech and sound, make sure to hire a production manager who is. This is probably the single most important role at a festival. If the sound sucks, nobody will be happy, even if you're in an amazing space with very good hummus.

Pharmakon performing in a bookstore

45

Also, hire a good sound person. If you don't know a sound person or anyone who can help with tech riders, and you're starting to get nervous about all of this, then hire a production company. You can stick to your role as "curator," and they'll do all the other stuff.

You have the venue lined up, the staff in place, and the lineup booked... now you need to figure out how you'll sell tickets. Will they be online only? Will people be able to get them at the door? Both? You'll also need

"Think of yourself as a curator, not just someone mindlessly adding all the 'big' bands in any given genre or scene."

to set the price so you don't lose your shirt. The price will be affected by whether or not you have sponsors. This is another big question: Do you want sponsors, which can make life easier, but can also be a pain in the ass? Or do you want to do it without sponsors, which can be stressful, but can also give you more control in the end? Up to you.

Once all of this is set, you'll need to promote the festival on social media. You may also want to organize a street team to hang up physical flyers. Even with the internet, these are still really useful. As the festival date gets closer, switch up your promotional tactics a bit so people still pay attention. If you use the same approach each time, it's easy for people to tune it out. See if any of the artists are up to tweeting the info or doing interviews. Speaking of which, if you have the money, you may want to hire a publicist.

Final tip: Don't drink when you're putting on a show. If someone needs your help, and you're a sloppy mess, things won't end well. By the end of the event, most folks will likely be wasted. They'll need you. Stay the course!

All said, it comes down to controlling the things you can control, and dealing with (or working around) the things you can't. Like, for instance, the weather. What if it rains for the entire event and you're doing it outdoors? Did you think ahead and get a tent for over the stage? Did you provide ponchos? That's the tip of the iceberg. Bands will have vans that break down. People will get lost.

People will have meltdowns. People will have bass amps that explode (maybe more than once, speaking from memorable experience). People will shit themselves on stage and keep playing (another true story). And when this kind of thing happens, you'll be standing there, smile on your face, knowing you did the best you could do, and that things will all be OK. And then you'll tell the band it's up to them to clean up that shit and you'll go home and go to sleep. ✍

BRANDON STOSUY *is the former director of editorial operations at Pitchfork. He now works at Kickstarter and books shows around the world.*

HEALTH, Viet Cong and White Lung perform at Basilica Soundscape, 2015. Photos By Samantha Marble

47

Phish Shreds America

How the Jam Band Anticipated Modern Festival Culture

By Jesse Jarnow
Illustrations by Matteo Berton

THE GREAT WENT. LIMESTONE, MAINE, AUGUST 1997. PHOTO BY BILL STITES

In the viral video that became known as "What Phish Sounds Like to People Who Don't Like Phish," the Vermont jam band performs in front of a field of cheering fans. So far, so Phish. But when the camera points at the bassist, only random diddles are heard. The players' parts are disconnected and small. The frontman emits gibberish. "You ate my fractal," he sings obscurely, in a doofed voice, like a "South Park" character.

Originally titled "Phish Shreds IT," the 2010 video was merely the latest iteration of the "shreds" meme, all of which feature images of bands performing live set to awkwardly strange audio. But the Phish video was the first time the joke had been used in this way, to explain how an oft-reviled band might sound to non-fans. Which suggested that Phish's popularity is so bizarre, so odious, that their music is the type of nonsense that makes one's brain throb.

The "IT" in "Phish Shreds IT" refers to their 2003 one-band mega-festival, during which Phish played seven sets over three days in front of over 60,000 fans (counting the all-jam set atop an air traffic control tower but not counting the soundcheck broadcast only heard over their on-site FM station). Typical for Phish, IT was held on a decommissioned Air Force base deep into northeastern Maine. Good, the Phish non-likers might assert, out of sight, out of mind.

But getting out of sight and out of mind are surely goals for many Phishheads, and the entire experience of escaping reality is built into the idea of their festival world. Since Phish's Clifford Ball in 1996, on another Air Force base near the band's Burlington, Vermont home, long-haul drives have been built into their festival aesthetic. On the eve of the millennium, they staged their furthest-fuckin'-out event, in Florida, sending 80,000 attendees down Alligator Alley in the Everglades, literally out of the boundaries of the United States—via an 18-hour zone-crossing traffic jam—and into Seminole Indian territory, where the band played an eight-hour midnight-to-sunrise set.

In all cases, what listeners found at the far end of their trips was a world where Phish's music made complete sense. Call it Stockholm syndrome or a unified artistic vision, but there's no denying that Phish built an audience and a platform of their own. With vast tracts for campers, playful large-scale installations designed by Vermont comrades connected to the radical Bread and Puppet Theater, unannounced late-night sets, an on-site freeform radio station, food vendors, Porta Potty (and sometimes art installations made from Porta Potty), it was a ready-to-go template that the band staged year after year in the late 1990s and sporadically since. Just as Phish's music might seem alien, their festival strategy was marked by the reverse of normal music-biz logic: Instead of picking central locations for their events, the band picked destinations seemingly as far away as possible. It wasn't merely live music, but a contract to enter Tent City, U.S.A., for the duration of the experience.

In the go-go indie '90s, Phish were among the indie-est of them all, even if they weren't exactly rock music as many wished to understand it. While they remained on a major label from 1991 until 2004, it was neither Elektra nor the band's album sales that propelled them to sell out multiple nights at Madison Square Garden. Phish's most popular and compelling music was distributed for free by the band's fans, and always had been. By the time of IT in 2003, as the music industry exploded into the blogosphere, Phishheads graduated from cassettes to mp3s and CD-Rs, and soon provided the critical mass to get BitTorrent off the ground, while Phish themselves graduated to selling recordings of all of their shows online within hours of the performance.

Night after night, through improvisation and song-suites, Phish changed in ways both micro and macro, creating new content on a near-daily basis while on tour. Each time Phish plays, fans have new bits of close-listening improv to dissect, new bits of folklore to trade, new bits of themselves to actualize. While there was (and is) a jam hit parade of sorts, a different economy drives the modern live music world that Phish helped create: part drama, part novelty, part boogie, and filled with extreme levels of detail to be pored over later.

All of which is to say that Phish were pipers at the dawn of America's 21st century festival revival, direct precursors to Bonnaroo, and early builders of an underground railway that eventually led to the collision of dance, jam, and indie subcultures in the vast common ground of the non-metaphoric concert field. While it would be an exaggeration to say that they were responsible for the endless crossovers of the festival circuit, they unquestionably nurtured an audience hungry for constantly changing live music outside the traditional mechanisms of the recording industry.

———

When the members of Phish enrolled at the experimental Goddard College, they were a bunch of suburban Deadheads in a far-flung spot in the counter-cultural empire. Starting primarily as a Grateful Dead cover band, Phish eventually traded in for a repertoire of original music refined during long Vermont winters, long green summers, long practice sessions, and long

weekly gigs in Burlington, where they built a hungry audience. The songs followed their own rhythmic muses and logic, a self-conscious attempt at creating a new kind of dance music, filled with palindromes, atonal fugues, and enough classic rock riffs and swing to keep hippies moving. It is here that Phish turns to gibber-ish for most people, for their insistence on fun, for the levels of expression coded therein.

But despite the band's oft-precious oddness, this is also why the giant multi-day campout-style music festival remains the musical platform in which Phish make the most sense. It is here that the band fully reconciles their extreme playfulness with the soaring guitar solos that arc through the summer air, over the rolling Vermont hills, and directly into memories. For those inclined to pay attention (and Phish fans do), there's a lot to pay attention to, though the drugs certainly contribute.

"The internet is to the Phish community what FM radio was for me back in the early '70s," Great Northeast Productions promoter Dave Werlin told Pollstar about collaborating with Phish to stage the biggest indie rock fests of the '90s. It's a sentiment many would voice over the years, except that Werlin said it in 1999, on the verge of Phish's millennium shows in Florida, and barely six months after Napster arrived to disrupt the American music industry at large. Using internet-enabled fan-bases to create active feedback loops is a route many would come to exploit, but Phish and their Deadhead antecedents were there first, chilling.

As prescient as Phish's long-haul formula may have been, their festival success emerged in parallel with the '90s birth of large-scale microcultures, providing a Northeastern counterpart to the early American electronic dance music in the Midwest, the DIY desert adventures of Burning Man, and the swelling ranks of indie rock, to go alongside the post-SoundScan main-streaming of country and hip-hop. Artists in many of these worlds structured their careers around recorded

51

PHISH

CLIFFORD BALL. PLATTSBURGH, NY, AUGUST 1996. PHOTO BY EVAN LUCHESSI LEON

product and music videos, supplementing it with live appearances. Phish and their jammy ilk found places of their own that Woodstocks '94 and '99 seemed to miss entirely—funky, fuzzy destinations for specific musical communities, which reached full flower at their festivals. They picked up fans at New England boarding schools, frat houses, and liberal arts colleges alike; their shows were expected to be freethinking and generally apolitical zones, welcoming and loving to anyone who could tolerate the music.

———

The last time Great Northeast Productions put on a Phish festival, in 2004, it was a disaster in many ways, though it wasn't the promoter's fault. Heavy rains more or less destroyed the concert site before the fest even began, and the storms continued to batter the area. As cars pulled off in Vermont's Northeast Kingdom and hit the traditional zone-crossing traffic jam, the order came for Phish and Great Northeast Productions to tell people to turn around. The band's freeform radio station interrupted their all-night fun with a taped bummer from Phish bassist Mike Gordon. Fans were now faced with a moral choice about whether to listen to the stated wishes of their favorite band or to ignore them and trek on at their own peril. Compounding the decision-making was the fact that Phish had announced their impending breakup three months earlier.

An estimated 65,000 of 70,000 ticket buyers made it in, some weathering cross-country drives, 36-hour traffic stints, and 15-mile hikes to the concert grounds. These shows—a festival called Coventry in Vermont's Northeast Kingdom in August 2004—would be the band's final performances. In the blooming age of cross-platform storytelling and common-sense money-making, the shows

were to be beamed out into movie theaters nationwide as well. In the midst of all of this, and almost certainly near the heart of the band's decision to disband, were the substance abuse issues that had crept up among them, making the wheels come off the bus even as they continued to go 'round and 'round.

Coventry was the type of legitimately emotional performance that doesn't often occur in popular music. There were mid-song tears, musical collapses, a few hot jams, and a palpably odd energy, all amid a boulder-strewn stage set designed to prevent further mudslides.

"We're not about to do a free-form jazz exploration in front of a festival crowd," David St. Hubbins barked in *This Is Spinal Tap*, but Phish built themselves a platform to do exactly that. In terms of the possibility of artistic creation afforded by a music festival, Coventry represented one possibility pushed to near-total bleakness. "Worst goodbye ever," read one fan-made T-shirt featuring Comic Book Guy from "The Simpsons." But it was powerful art. Though the band kept playing their familiar songs, their world had broken down, and it showed no signs of ever making sense again.

This particular Phish festival likewise came during the dawn of the new festival season. One true and deep characteristic of festivals, going back at least to Woodstock, was a guaranteed escape. If a giant news event occurred somewhere out yonder, it might only arrive in Tent City via rumor. Cell phones hit ubiquity around the time of IT and Coventry, but all-access internet hadn't yet landed; a trip to northern Vermont could be coordinated, but when the shit hit the fans and the band had to tell people to go home, it came by short-range FM radio.

53

Phish were pipers at the dawn

of America's 21st century

festival revival, direct precursors

to Bonnaroo, and early builders

of an underground railway

that eventually led to the

collision of dance, jam, and

indie subcultures.

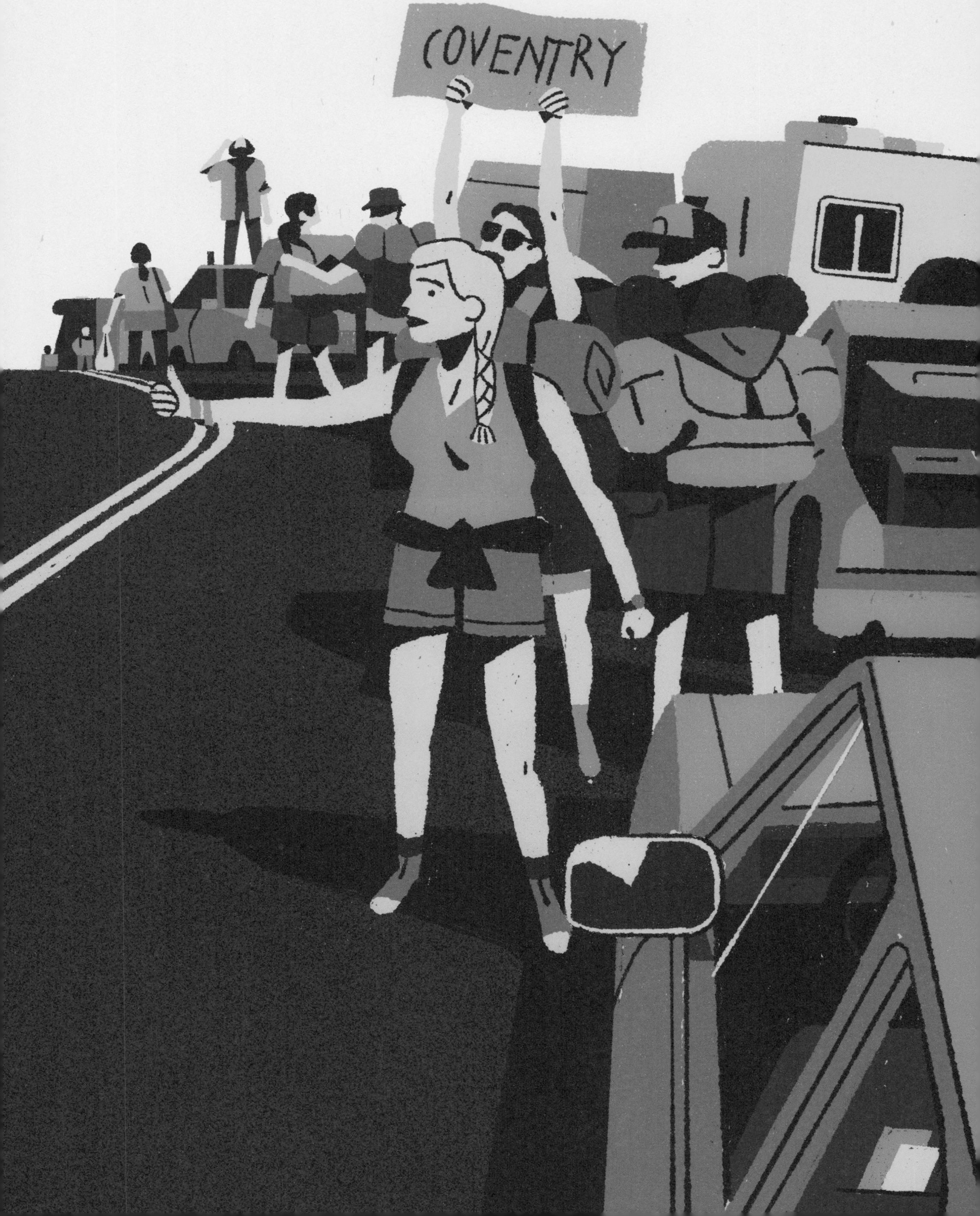
COVENTRY

TOP: CLIFFORD BALL. PLATTSBURGH, NY, AUGUST 1996. PHOTO BY EVAN LUCHESSI LEON
BOTTOM: THE GREAT WENT. LIMESTONE, MAINE, AUGUST 1997. PHOTO BY BILL STITES

By the time Phish reformed in 2009, accepting a slower pace, they sounded like themselves again, crisp and filled with detailed rhythmic punchlines and long-form musical narratives. But the festival world had shifted around them, turning into a national circuit for bands of all genres. First staged in 2002, Bonnaroo—built on the jammy networks that Phish had nurtured—spread into nearly every musical territory imaginable, surfing an even bigger audience by tapping into jam fans' open-mindedness toward fun-compliant live acts.

While Phish occasionally show up to play many-band extravaganzas, they are content to stick to themselves, too, and continue to stage their own festivals from time to time. But when they do—as in 2015's Magnaball, population ~30,000—the events continue to tap into something that most festivals of equivalent size miss. While jam/electronic getaways like Camp Bisco and Electric Forest have their roots in the Phish world, Phish's closest modern kin are perhaps more easily found in smaller fan-friendly events like the improv/avant-friendly Big Ears in Knoxville, with an emphasis on the intimate musical experience, even at scale. Lately, Phish have moved into luxury destination territory, having announced their second visit to a Mexican resort for 2017, though Phish fans—both recovering and active—have long constituted a reliable pocket of attendees at places like Big Ears and the earlier, more functional American iterations of All Tomorrow's Parties.

In many ways, it's a formula that few rock festivals have repeated because few have really tried: the creation of a space for absolute hyper-focused listening with the performance of the musicians at the unquestionable fixed center. Besides the advent of VIP camping and a few ticket-pricing confusions, perhaps the most controver-sial aspect of MagnaBall among Phish fans was whether or not the improvisation that followed "Prince Caspi-an" constituted a return to the song "Tweezer" or was merely reminiscent of it.

Though with unquestionable countercultural roots, Phish generated an entirely different set of parameters and concerns from the lamplight of Coachella, the active participation of Burning Man, the something-for-everybody parties of Outside Lands and elsewhere, the surf and turf deliciousness of JazzFest, the blissed-out multi-day electronic dance-outs, the yoga bend-ins, and even the so-called transformational festivals that have spread across Europe. Phish festivals aren't about counterculture or psychedelics or even the vaunted community. They are about music—a hilarious, cruel, or absolutely fitting punchline that's far funnier than any viral video could possibly convey. ✍

57

JESSE JARNOW *is a writer and DJ on WFMU. He recently published* Heads: A Biography of Psychedelic America.

For those who like to read but maybe not all the time...

Comics!

THIS LITTLE PREFORMANCE PIECE IS KINDA BACED AROUND THE MISFORTUNES OF DESIRE

OF WHICH I'M CHRONICALLY PLAGUED

OFTEN ACTED OUT IN THIS IMAGINARY LANDSCAPE OF SEAMLESS ABUNDANCE

BUT ALWAYS DEGENERATING EVENTRUALLY INTO A SERIES OF HOSTILE LIES

AND I'M SO DAMN SICK OF HOSTILITY

WE FALL AGAIN AND AGAIN, ALWAYS SEARCHING BLINDLY FOR THE LIBERATION OF RELIEF

RELIEF FROM THIS RAT RACE

THIS FUCKING HUMAN RAT RACE

WE'RE ALL EXILED FROM TRUTH AND FORCE FED SO MANY GOD DAMN LIES WE NOT ONLY START TO BEILEVE THE LIES BUT PROPAGATE THE LIES

LIKE MILLIONS OF POMPOUS CORPSES

BY TOMMI PARRISH — WORDS RIFFING OFF A LYDIA LUNCH POEM

TOMMI PARRISH

FESTIVAL LOOKBOOK 2055

BE ANYONE YOU WANT TO BE. THE HOLO-CLOAK PROJECTS CONFIDENCE!

CAGE-FREE VENUSIAN SENTIENT WIGS WERE BRED TO MAKE YOU BEAUTIFUL

STEP INTO ROOT BOOTS TO PHOTOSYNTHESIZE AFTER A LONG DAY IN THE SUN

SOAR HIGH ABOVE THE CROWD IN A PTERODACTYL FLIGHT SUIT...

OR PUT ON A SENSORY DEPRIVATION SUIT TO GET AWAY FROM IT ALL.

STIMULATE YOUR PRE-FRONTAL CORTEX WITH BRAINFRAMES™ FOR AN ENHANCED AUDIO-VISUAL EXPERIENCE

LEATHER SPACE FEST

THE BAND IMMEDIATELY STOOD OUT FROM THE REST OF THE FESTIVAL ACTS. FROM THE AUDIENCE, TOO. WE HAD BAGGY SHIRTS, STRINGY HAIR, TORN JEANS... A LOT OF PLAID, OF COURSE

THEIR FIRST SET WAS DAY ONE, EARLY AFTERNOON. THERE WAS RAIN. IT WAS SPARSELY ATTENDED BUT WELL RECEIVED

IT WAS DURING THE CANKERS' SET THAT WE BEGAN TO NOTICE THE CHANGE TAKE PLACE. THEIR BASSIST LOOKED A LITTLE DRESSIER THAN USUAL. HIS PLAYING HAD CHANGED TOO - TIGHTER, MORE FEROCIOUS

BY THAT EVENING, AT LEAST ONE MEMBER OF EVERY BAND ON THE BILL HAD BEEN CONVERTED

ON THE FINAL DAY OF THE FESTIVAL, THE CROWD HAD FULLY TRANSFORMED. NOT A SINGLE BAGGY SHIRT IN SIGHT. THE LEATHER SPACE BAND PLAYED THEIR SECOND SET TO A PACKED AUDIENCE AT 10:30 PM, SUNDAY NIGHT

MICHAEL DEFORGE

Not Just Another Picnic in the Park

FOR NEARLY A DECADE, THE ROOTS PICNIC HAS BEEN A MODEL FOR ARTIST-CURATED FESTIVALS DONE RIGHT. AS THE PHILADELPHIA EVENT EXPANDS TO NEW YORK CITY THIS FALL, QUESTLOVE EXPLAINS HIS WINNING STRATEGY.

By Jace Clayton

GOOD DRUMMERS KNOW THAT TIME IS PLASTIC. THE BEAT MUST GO ON, BUT YOU CAN PLAY AHEAD OF IT OR BEHIND IT, MAKE IT SWING OR SWITCH UP THE TUNE ENTIRELY.

Drumming is a heartbeat art, concerned with music at its most elemental: questions of momentum, time, sound, and space. Ahmir "Questlove" Thompson has devoted his life to reinventing what a beatmaker can do. He got his start tapping out bucket rhythms on Philadelphia street corners and has steadily worked to become America's most iconic drummer. Some know him as the guy in the Roots who leads TV's coolest in-house band on "The Tonight Show"; others recognize him as a key architect of the late 1990s neo-soul sound of D'Angelo and Erykah Badu. A cultural omnivore, lately his bold-name dinner parties, featuring some of the best chefs on the planet, have become the stuff of foodie legend. And wherever he pops up, you can't miss Quest: He stands at a hefty six-foot-four, and that's before you factor in the Afro and hair-pick.

Questlove's work spearheading the annual Roots Picnic provides the best way to think about what his unique sensibilities look like writ large. Since 2008, the fest has brought eclectic lineups to Quest's native Philadelphia, and this October the one-day affair expands to a two day concert at New York City's Bryant Park. Even amid the drummer and DJ's constant flurry of activity, the event is a big moment for this tireless artist, whose work ethic becomes even more impressive when you meet him—how can a man with such a full plate be so funny and relaxed?

TPR **Why did you want to start your own festival in the first place?**

Q The genesis of it all was when I went to Japan in '97 and picked up all sorts of concert footage. At that point in life, I literally was YouTube. Especially during the *Voodoo* sessions with D'Angelo, I was carrying these large Kipling bags full of nothing but videotapes and DVDs of performances you couldn't find anywhere. One of those performances I always held dear was an event called the Police Picnic, which happened in Toronto every year between '81 and '83. Each member of the Police curated each night, and the lineup was really diverse, from the Specials to B.B. King to P-Funk All Stars. Now America has finally caught onto festival culture—it's not close to Europe but at least there's a good 20 to 30 festivals going on in the United States that are worth making a pilgrimage to—and I think it's more special when artists curate them.

What did you want to bring to Philadelphia when you started the Roots Picnic there nine years ago?

You gotta understand: Around that time, the City of Brotherly Love was flirting with being the city with the highest murder rate in the United States of America. And I always felt like we owed Philly something. I don't mean something like, *Here's a token gesture Philly, thanks for all of the support, see ya.* The dream always was to pay it forward. It's not like the festival is going to change the world or have the same impact as Coachella or Bonnaroo, but doing that one small gesture a year makes us feel like we're doing our part giving back to the city of Philadelphia.

In the beginning, we did it without sponsors—and these things cost a lot of money. And we insist on keeping the ticket under $100. I wanted something very affordable, very accessible. For some of these acts, we'd talk them down from the normal price: "Come on, Animal Collective, you guys need 12 cases of wine?" That's a hypothetical—I don't want people thinking that Animal Collective had 12 cases of wine! I just mean that you have to be seriously hands-on and call a lot of these acts that you meet throughout life and explain to them that this is for a bigger cultural cause.

What do you think makes musical festivals important for musicians?

Every musician wants to think that he's gonna have this legendary Woodstock moment. But for Jimi Hendrix, I'm sure Woodstock was just like, "Oh, that's Sunday. I gotta go on at five in the morning? Fuck." With the Roots, for a lot of our magical moments, the further and more obscure the festival, the more ass-kicking it's been, so my thought is that people's enthusiasm grows when they have less access to music or festivals. And if that theory is correct, then we might be troubled at Bryant Park! Which is why we're going all out to make this more than just your average random lineup of six acts you heard of and 20 acts you haven't.

As a curator, how are you approaching the New York Roots Picnic?

Our egos definitely want to do a slam dunk where the backboard comes off the rim with this one. Initially, everybody except Barack Obama was gonna perform a song onstage, and I was just like, "This is too good. We're setting ourselves up

67

"EVERY MUSICIAN WANTS TO THINK THAT HE'S

GONNA HAVE THIS LEGENDARY WOODSTOCK

MOMENT. BUT FOR JIMI HEDRIX, I'M SURE

WOODSTOCK WAS JUST LIKE, 'OH, THAT'S SUNDAY.

I GOTTA GO ON AT FIVE IN THE MORNING? FUCK.'"

to not be as powerful next year." So we decided to hammer down a concept, which stopped the overflow. The first night is going to be reminiscent of our jam sessions back in ['90s NYC club] Wetlands, where anybody would come up onstage and occasionally some magic would go down. So, I felt like if we just advertised two strong names and a supergroup with D'Angelo and John Mayer—and then still booked a lot of acts that we won't advertise, as a surprise thing—that's magic in itself. The goal of that night is to create an intimate atmosphere. It's hard to do that in front of 15,000 people but, we're gonna try.

The next night we're dubbing our love letter to New York City, with some really iconic New York artists from all walks of life: Wu-Tang, David Byrne, and Nile Rodgers, and then a slew of unannounced guests will join onstage. My only worry is that I have yet to do a New York show and really enjoy it because of the fact that I'm also the traffic cop and referee. No one knows the pain of when it's 10:59 p.m. and you know the second that it hits 11 p.m. [curfew officials] are looking at you like, "You know it's $16,000 right?" I got to figure out how to plan the perfect two-hour show where the audience feels as though they got their money's worth and the artist feels it was worth coming down.

For some reason, we waited nine years to see if New York even wanted a part of this. A lot of it was just in my head: I thought there would be too much red tape, too many headaches. Then one day my manager was like, "Why don't we just ask?" And much to my surprise we sent them an email, and they came back full force like, "When do you want to do it? What park do you want?" We were like, "Slow down!" We were shocked that they were so open and welcoming.

As the Roots Picnic grows, how do you plan to maintain that spirit of making a special moment?
I want people to know that we are personally involved—I'm calling D'Angelo, I'm calling John Mayer. It's not just like,

"Hey Live Nation, can you get Beyoncé for us?" One of the other ways I figure we could make this really special was to incorporate other areas of entertainment other than music in the future: DJ tents, food tents, comedy tents, movie tents. So Bryant Park is a testing period, and if we can prove that we do good business and that we're culturally on-point, then I think the doors will open.

Everything you're doing has a fair amount of discovery in it. What's your secret to finding the new thing?
You should never be the smartest person in your crew. In my circle, we're a bunch of smart asses, and smart asses are always trying to one-up each other—I'm constantly at the receiving end of someone's one-upmanship, and I welcome it. ✏

69

JACE CLAYTON *is a writer and, as DJ Rupture, a musician.*

Burning Man's Forgotten Visionaries

By Daniel Martin-McCormick

The drive by shooting range, 1992

71

Thirty years later, does
the lawless desert
retreat still remember its
experimental roots?

Photo by Kimric Smythe

I s it possible to say that a 30-year-old festival that annually attracts nearly 70,000 people—including celebrities like P. Diddy, Katy Perry, and Kate Moss—has a cult following? Before Burning Man became the international phenomenon it is today, the survivalist-cum-art-installation was simply "Zone Trip #4 - Bad Day at Black Rock," a 1990 Labor Day camping trip for 80 or so members of San Francisco's free spirited Cacophony Society. Inspired by Ken Kesey's Merry Pranksters, the network of friends and artists used San Francisco as a canvas for, in their own words, "absurdist escapades." Typical events included cocktail parties in the sewer, elegant dinners on the Golden Gate Bridge, and conceptual group journeys called Zone Trips.

Carrie Galbraith conceived that last idea. Having joined the Cacophony Society in 1986 while studying art, she was a passionate believer in the group's ideals of experimentation and noncommercial expression. "Andrei Tarkovsky made a [1979] film called *Stalker*, all about getting into a 'Zone.' What happens in the Zone is totally different than your own reality, and anything goes," she says today. "The concept behind the Zone Trip was that once you stepped over the line, all bets from your normal world are off and you have to work with the confines of a new reality." The rules of this new reality were to keep the events not-for-profit and participatory: "The only thing we ever said is you can't make money off of it. You charge admission only if you need to recoup your expenses."

Zone Trip #4 was originally planned as a camping weekend with a smattering of performances and group activities, but a budding collaboration with two friends named Larry Harvey and Jerry James would lead to a notable addition. Four years earlier, in 1986, Harvey and James took over an annual summer solstice bonfire run on San Francisco's Baker Beach. The event was small, only for a handful of friends, but for their inaugural edition, they decided to build and burn an eight-foot effigy. The reasons behind this are disputed—one rumor claims the figure represented Harvey's ex-girlfriend—but the monument was undeniably spectacular. By 1990, several hundred spectators were convening on Baker Beach for the sculpture's fiery destruction, now dubbed the Burning Man.

Having grown to 40 feet tall, the Man inevitably attracted the attention of law enforcement, who shut down the unlicensed event. Meanwhile, Cacophony members Kevin Evans and John Law were already organizing Zone Trip #4, a retreat inspired by their recent excursions to the Black Rock Desert in northwestern Nevada. "It was this gigantic open canvas in which you could place, or do, anything," recalls Evans, noting how experiences in the vast expanse "became magnified because of the nothingness of the place." He suggested relocating the effigy there.

Within a year, the Zone Trip was rebranded as Burning Man and the festival's atmosphere began to take shape. In one of the most inhospitable and unregulated places in North America, a wild-eyed, playful, and willfully bizarre art culture grew. Attendees donned costumes, dressing as Santa and serving eggnog in oppressive heat and played polo on mountain bikes between sandstorms. Alter egos emerged, like Java Cow, an elusive character created by pyrotechnician Kimric Smythe who served black coffee and satirical quips to stragglers and curiosity-seekers at dawn. The concept of "Leave No Trace" became a mantra, wherein attendees attempted to preserve and protect the natural state of the site.

As Burning Man evolved, tensions over money, ownership, and purpose quickly flared up. In 1991, Harvey began advertising the event beyond the inner circle of the Cacophony Society, with a ticket price of $15. (Other attendees report that, upon arrival to the desert, now dubbed the Playa, Harvey charged them $35.) These admission fees went against core Cacophony Society principles and caused a significant divide within the organization.

W e tracked down early participants who were partly responsible for building the festival and shaping its direction, many still living in the Bay Area. (Harvey and other longtime organizers still working for Burning Man declined to comment.) For some, the early years repre-

Photo by Kimric Smythe

73

Pyroman performance, 1993

Top: Kevin Evans & Sebastian Hyde's camp with the Cacophony Society's 5:04 p.m. Earthquake Car, 1991
Bottom: The Man, Down, 1990

sented a youthful utopia that was probably too good to last. For others, there's a lingering anger that their ideals and work were exploited and corrupted: In 2016, tickets range from $390 to $1200, and Burning Man has become a household name—albeit one synonymous with hallucinogenic decadence, flaky New-Age-isms, and questionable fashion choices. Though transformed into something apparently unrecognizable to many of its original adherents, its first decade's radical ideals and interpersonal battle lines still resonate, the echoes and artifacts of a truly underground movement.

Early Trips to the Black Rock Desert: "They Thought We Were Satanists"

Carrie Galbraith, *who conceived the Zone Trip experience.* We didn't call it a festival. It didn't even really have a name. And we put it in our [Cacophony Society] newsletter, probably from 1987 to 1990, saying, "Hey, let's all meet at the beach and burn the Man," or burn a man. We didn't call it the Man.

Dan Miller, *a close friend of Harvey and James, was present at the solstice bonfire in 1986. Since then, he's attended every Burning Man, working with the festival until 2000.* Going out there in those earlier times, it was dangerous. You can disappear out there. It's 400-square miles, just the Playa itself, let alone the mountains. You break down, or run out of water... people die out there.

You can go out and basically pedal to the metal, over 100 miles-per-hour and recline in your seat and take a nap. That's what we did. It's open space, forever.

Former street kid and key Burning Man artist **Kal Spelletech** *worked with Survival Research Laboratories, a machine-performance group that channeled political rage into immersive, confrontational events throughout the 1980s. For example, the collective staged battles among fire-breathing robots—often outfitted with animal carcasses and evoking a looming industrial-military dystopia—in remote Bay Area locations. Though SRL would never collec-*

tively attend or perform at Burning Man, many SRL alumni would become integral members of the festival's growing pyrotechnics wing and would carry the unsettling outlaw aesthetic into the Black Rock Desert. [Burning Man] was hard to find, to be honest. You had these vague directions and you'd just drive out into this barren desert where you couldn't see anything. And you'd bring a compass. It was like, "Go north by northeast, drive 11 miles, and eventually you'll see some settlement." Often [directions] would be like, "At mile six, slow down because there's some holes in the desert and people are breaking their axles if they're going too fast."

Carrie Galbraith [Burning Man had] a really strong sense of fraternity. We were in a remote location, and the Black Rock was really remote then. Gerlach [the only town nearby] was a gas station and a diner and a grocery store, and they were in one building. And a bar. They thought we were Satanists.

Bill Smythe, *first went to Burning Man in 1992 in his early 60s. The father of Java Cow-performer Kimric Smythe, he saw an opportunity to connect with his son and to explore a late-in-life interest in art.* I'm not much of an artist; I was just curious to see what the heck was going on. I drove up in a Mercedes-Benz that was relatively new. My wife was not happy about it. They were out there shooting guns—most all of us brought guns just to play around with—and it was just a bunch of tents.

Cacophony society member Kevin Evans helped to organize Zone Trip #4 after attending a wind sculpture festival in the Black Rock Desert in 1989. Although he would attend Burning Man for years, he recalls the first trips to the desert with a particular nostalgia.

You gotta understand we were all broke artists. We did what we could. My friend Sebastian and I were slathered in the Playa mud, walking around as primitives.

William Binzen *is the founder of Desert Siteworks, an art collective that conducted smaller artistic retreats to the Black Rock Desert concurrently with Burning Man.* In the early days, Burning Man was a very disorganized, very disheveled group of folks who were kinda confused.

75

"By 2000 or 2001, Burning Man was just a bunch of fucked-up wahoos. You might as well be at a rock concert."

—Kal Spelletech

Well, we're out here now, we ought to do something. It was really a three-day tailgate party, a lot of people just hanging around, drinking beer, with small fires at night. Then we burned the Man.

Carrie Galbraith

In those days, everybody who was there helped raise the Man. He was just a part of it. The whole event was about people getting together and camping in the desert and doing whatever they wanted to do. It wasn't because of the Burning Man.

Playa Experiments: "We Had a Barney Execution"

Bill Smythe

I got a bunch of big fancy [children's] toys from the local Goodwill, and then I went up there and used ski poles, put them in the ground and tied these things in place [for a firing range]. You would drive down the road and fire out the window and shoot at these things. My main problem was trying to keep people from shooting across the road. I said, "The Feds could put you in jail." They were high on something.

Kimric Smythe *was not only the man behind Java Cow, but also a pyrotechnician who worked closely with Burning Man as it grew in scope and ambition. In addition to rigging an increasingly complex network of fireworks and combustible materials to the Man, he would perform with flammables attached to his body.*

We had some giant stuffed bear about 100 yards out, for long range shooting. [Also, there was a] whole zone of nothing but Barneys We had a Barney execution.

Kal Spelletech

I first went in 1995. I wouldn't go earlier because these guys were such dorks and weirdos and nerds. I was working with SRL and we were doing flamethrowers and giant machines. They want to have a bonfire on the beach. It's like, "Oh, that's cute."

Kimric Smythe

It was sort of a secret who the actual Java Cow was. It started out serious, but I realized it was inherently funny, and so I ran with the comedic aspect of it. We had the whole thing of "Do you want cream and sugar in your coffee?" and everybody had to declare "No, we like it black." And then I started going on about not falling into the evil ways of the De-Calf, who was the false god, or the Coffee Maid, its evil minion. It would get 30 people showing up, people staying up all night hoping to see the Java Cow.

Friction and Financial Disputes: "Sorry, We Brought Our Own Chemical Toilet"

Carrie Galbraith

[The second year] was pretty much the same. The only difference is that we were approached [by Burning Man organizers] and asked for money. We were like, "What? Sorry, we brought our own chemical toilet. This is Bureau of Land Management land, our taxes pay for it. I'm not going to pay you for the privilege of being out here." And that was when I first saw the head of the monster rise.

William Binzen

One of the times I was in [San Francisco] visiting [Larry Harvey], we were sitting in his kitchen and drinking coffee. He said, "Bill, I know you're into sacred geometry and metaphysical things. What do you think we should do for designing this camp?" Because it was just as if you threw socks and shoes together on the floor. I drew a target and a cross dividing the target into four quadrants. I oriented the cross with the compass and then I said we should create a clock based on this target that allows us to also be in relationship with the four directions. We should have a large sundial in the center that will enable us to tell the time of day. In the center we would have our circle where everyone would come together. And let's put the man outside the circle and off at some distance along a pathway, which I compared with a pilgrimage route. We'll have a ritual performance that will involve everybody from the camp coming together and forming a group and walking out to the man and we can have further ritual actions there.

The reason for putting the man outside the circle is that we don't want to engage in any form of idolatry, the creation of some sort of object which takes on a quasi-sacred cast.

77

Loading a dead VW into the back of the moving truck that brought the
Burning Man sculpture out to the Black Rock, 1990

Cacophony Members inspect the camp location, 1990

Photos by Hyde/Serxl

He took all these ideas, with the exception of the placement of the man. I have always felt that Larry put the man in the center because the man was an extension of his ego. He said, "Bill, I see a million people on the Playa."

John Law *was deeply involved in the Cacophony Society and, along with Kevin Evans, scouted the location for the first Zone Trip to the desert. He worked closely with Harvey on Burning Man through 1996, after which point unresolvable differences caused him to leave the festival in disgust.*

Infusing this empty symbol with such power was disturbing to me. I, and others, had constantly come up with different ideas for mocking the central symbol of the Man. The original spirit of the Cacophony Society was to poke fun at the hypocrisies and stupidity of society.

At different times we had hoped to build a burning dog, maybe make the man upside down, or have him on one leg with a crutch. The whole idea of this community and this experiment was to stand against the conformity and top-down hierarchy one tends to find in cities.

Rapid Population Growth: "Like Hell for Reality"

By 1995, Burning Man's attendance was approximately 4,000. The next year, with "The Inferno" as its theme, that number would double. With so many people in an unregulated space, injuries and death were inevitable. In 1996, neon contractor Michael Furey died in a motorcycle accident on the Playa. It was the first death at Burning Man.

John Law

In 1994 [festival co-organizer] Michael Mikel, Larry Harvey, and I founded a business partnership to own the Burning Man event. By 1996, it was clear that the event was either going to end or grow into a massive, popular festival. There was no third path.

I felt we were incapable of safely carrying out the event. We had little or no money; we were in debt from mismanagement. Neither Michael, Larry, nor myself had any clue how to run an actual business. The phrase "Leave No Trace," which had been largely true for the first few years, was now becoming a mere PR statement. By 1996, our cleanup was not sufficient at all. We were not only 'leaving a trace,' we were actually causing a great deal of environmental disruption by introducing thousands and thousands of people to this remote place.

Kimric Smythe

[In 1996] we had a heaven-and-hell theme, and it kinda became a mental meltdown—too much like hell for reality. We made this mini volcano in the middle of the camp and had all these plaster faces that had all these different half-assed excuses about why you had done the things you did written on them, and they were circling the volcano. And we had these great demon knight helmets we had made and these costumes. It was supposed to be an elevator to hell.

That year too I burned my hand really badly and had to go to the hospital. I was loading a mortar, and it's so dry out there that static set off the black powder and blew all the skin off my hand. I had to go into Reno and get my hand debrided and come back out and finish rigging the pyro. So I'm rigging the pyro with my left hand and the audience grabs the robe and hauls the Man up, and partly drags me off the ground with my remaining hand. I just about punched one of the people in the line.

I used to do Pyroman, where I would wear about 25 pounds of fireworks... We would wear these giant pinwheels and walk around with stuff flying all over the place.

Bill Smythe

When, Kimric burnt his hand badly, I had to go out there and do the [Pyroman] dance with his ex-wife. We had pyrotechnics on our helmets and on our backs. It was wild. We would have helmets and big glasses and on top of the helmet you'd have a pinwheel that would spin. And you'd have a big fire wheel on your back, spinning like crazy.

Kimric had a full fireman's outfit on when the Man was burning. A couple times he ran out, and tackled people who were going to kill themselves by jumping into the Burning Man after it had fallen onto the ground.

The Furry Pants Crowd Arrives: "Boonk Boonk Boonk"

By the mid-to-late '90s, a growing contingent of DJs and ravers was trekking out to the Playa. A November '96 Wired

79

magazine cover story helped to bring word of Burning Man to an even wider audience, and many were disillusioned by the new, louder crop of attendees.

Kimric Smythe

I think the inclusion of the rave scene really brought in a lot of your spectator crowd. Burning Man wasn't about making money, but the raves are. So you had these people showing up with their equipment, using the Burning Man as a backdrop. It was the *Cat in the Hat* hat and the furry pants. The music was dominant, really oppressive, and nonstop. That drove me bonkers.

Kal Spelletech

I don't remember any rave [in the early days]. It would be friends' bands coming up from the city, but there wasn't the raver thing. By the late '90s, boy, that was annoying: listening to "Boonk boonk boonk" for two weeks and it wouldn't stop, it would go all night. Torture.

Bill Smythe

One thing we didn't like: some outfits had extraordinarily loud music. They'd show up every year and keep you awake until dawn. We threatened to blow their damn place up one time and almost had a fistfight with half a dozen guys. We finally got them to shut up.

Burning Man Today: "All Fancy Trailers or Motor Homes"

Dan Miller

The event is like a stone soup, where there's nothing there but what people bring.

Carrie Galbraith

By 1992, I walked away. I felt like Cacophony had been hijacked. Burning Man was a death knell for Cacophony—it sucked all the air out of the room. I just couldn't stomach co-opting Cacophony principles for profit.

Bill Smythe

Now when you go to the Man, it's all fancy trailers or motor homes. But, yeah, it was kinda nice. Young ladies walking around with not much on.

Kal Spelletech

[When I arrived] I had a big, old shit-eating grin. You see all your friends around and everyone's caked in dust and people are around bonfires. It's an incredible moment, so psychedelic and exciting and unknown—you feel like you're pioneering a new culture. By 2000 or 2001, it was just a bunch of fucked up wahoos. You might as well be at a rock concert.

Kimric Smythe

I don't think anybody knows what [Java Cow] is now. I remember trying to go back out and do it in, like, 2003? I'm standing out there trying to give people coffee, and nobody wants coffee. These burned out raver kids are giving you the side eye. We stood around for a while and then left. I'm walking through center camp, still in the Java Cow outfit, and some guy goes, "Hey it's really too early for this sort of thing." I walk up to the coffee counter in center camp and I go, "After all these years, the Java Cow would like a complimentary cup of coffee." And the girl just looks at me and she's like, "No. Next." ✐

DANIEL MARTINMCCORMICK *is a writer and musician who performs as Ital.*

Photos by Hyde/Segal

Morning Man, Burning Man, 1990

The Newport Jazz Festival

Few festivals have sustained the cultural impact of the Newport Jazz Festival. Established in 1954 as the First Annual American Jazz Festival, the Newport, Rhode Island mainstay is now inexorably linked with the genre and its legacy.

Aside from the consistently excellent performances—from legendary early sets by the likes of Miles Davis and Billie Holiday to this year's lineup, featuring Norah Jones and Kamasi Washington—Newport has always been representative of the cutting edge culture surrounding the music. It is as much a showcase for the music as it is a celebration of the past, present, and future of the genre. As Duke Ellington himself said, after an iconic performance in 1956 that found his audience standing on their chairs and dancing in the aisles, "I was born at the Newport Jazz Festival." Here's a look at those who came into the world the same way. —*Sam Sodomsky*

Louis Armstrong, 1958

Billie Holiday, 1957 / Miles Davis, 1969

Duke Ellington, 1968 / The Raelettes, 1967

Nina Simone, 1968 / John Coltrane, 1966

James Brown, 1969 / Tina Turner, 1970

Jimmy Smith, 1971 / Ella Fitzgerald, 1970

Aretha Franklin, 1973

George Benson, 1969

Ray Charles, 1972 / Diana Ross, 1974

Cool Like That

By Michael A. Gonzales

The Reunited Digable Planets Look Back

Photo by Michael Ochs Archives/Getty Images

In the same 1990s gangsta rap era that birthed the likes of Snoop Dogg, Wu-Tang, and Mobb Deep, a mild mannered trio called Digable Planets quietly emerged on the scene and, for a short time, burned bright on that acid-jazz vibe.

Looking like the younger cousins of De La Soul and A Tribe Called Quest, the group consisted of Seattle rapper and producer Ishmael "Butterfly" Butler—who named the group while reading though volumes of Jorge Luis Borges—along with East Coast MCs Mary Ann "Ladybug Mecca" Vieira and Craig "Doodlebug" Irving.

After first connecting over their love for jazz, poetry, and the street culture of hip-hop in 1991, the group soon began recording their debut album, *Reachin' (A New Refutation of Time and Space)*, in New York City. The record featured a sample of James Brown's immortal "Funky Drummer," and within a year of its February 1993 release, Digable were opening up for the iconic soul man on tour. Meanwhile, the album's effortlessly smooth, horn-laden single "Rebirth of Slick (Cool Like Dat)" became a Top 20 hit, eventually earning them a Grammy.

Things were going great, so of course it couldn't last. After their sophomore album *Blowout Comb* failed to repeat their initial success, the group splintered and its members started working on separate projects. After returning back home to Seattle, Butler formed Shabazz Palaces; Irving returned to his native Philadelphia and founded Cee Knowledge and the Cosmic Funk Orchestra; for the past six years, Vieira has been working on an ambitious project with producer Prince Paul that is scheduled for a fall release.

But now, 25 years after they initially got together, Digable are heading out on a U.S. tour this summer—including a stop at the Pitchfork Music Festival in Chicago—backed by a band that Butler compares to Earth, Wind & Fire. And though they have reunited for shows before, they are now even considering a return to the studio to record a new album. Here, all three members reminisce about their artistic beginnings and why their particular sensibilities came together so well.

TPR **How did you first meet each other?**

CRAIG "DOODLEBUG" IRVING   When I was at Howard University, I started hanging out with guys that were part of the Five-Percent Nation who were into partying and the hip-hop scene. Back then, I was DJing and had turntables set up in my room, made some beats. Ladybug was connected to that scene, and our relationship went from there.

ISHMAEL "BUTTERFLY" BUTLER   I was always seeing [Irving] around. He's from Philadelphia, where my father also lived, so I'd see him at the Penn Relays or at Howard's homecoming, and then again at the West Indian Parade in Brooklyn. We just ended up talking, and I found out he had a group in D.C. I was like, "Man, we should do some shit together." He knew Mecca and introduced her to me; we all ran together in D.C. and then we all lived together in Philly for about a year.

MARY ANN "LADYBUG MECCA" VIEIRA   When they started working together, they suggested I write a rhyme too. So I did, and their reaction was like, "Wow." They went upstairs and had a meeting, and when they came back

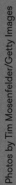

down, they asked me if I wanted to join the group. I'd always wanted to be in music, but until becoming a part of Digable Planets, that wasn't something I shared with everyone. When I was a kid, I would write my thoughts down on these small pieces of paper and stuff them in a grocery bag that hung on my door. I was an introvert.

IRVING Ish was the heart of Digable Planets, without a doubt, but we all had chops and brought something to the table that added to the flavor that made the group what it was.

What was it about Mecca's flow that made her right for Digable Planets?
BUTLER She had a certain off-beatness that was unique back then—a rhythmic approach and pronunciation of things that was just different. And though we'd all heard of Brazil, I didn't know any Brazilian females.

VIEIRA I grew up listening to Brazilian singers as well as Dakota Staton, Billie Holiday, and Sade. And listening to MC Lyte, Queen Latifah, and Roxanne Shanté gave me confidence and the strength to do it too. Those women weren't taking shit from anybody, and I was like that. When I was a kid I wasn't into Barbies or baby dolls, I was playing with G.I. Joes in the dirt with the boys.

In developing the Digable Planets sound, how did you decide to take the group in that jazzy funk direction that is so prominent on your debut?
BUTLER At the time, I wasn't thinking about musical categories. I was just using the samples that I could get my hands on; they were from records that belonged to my moms, my pops, and my uncles. My father was a stated jazz aficionado and he was into all the avant-garde stuff; he was a big

Eric Dolphy fan. Mom liked Motown and CTI jazz, Donald Byrd kind of stuff. That shit was fly too. My sound also came from what I was listening to: DJ Premier, Prince Paul, Cocteau Twins, P-Funk, Prince. A gumbo of all of that stuff became our sound.

After signing with Pendulum Records, the three of you moved to New York to work with producers Shane Faber and Mike Mangini. What was that experience like?
IRVING Ish already had the album laid out and knew how he wanted to do it, but the label decided [Faber and Mangini] would be the best production team to supervise the project. They had worked on some Native Tongues projects and helped us bring our vision to life. They had a studio in Bergen, New Jersey, and we'd take the dollar bus over there at 10 in the morning and work all day.

BUTLER We had a record coming out—that's all they had to tell me. I was so excited you would've thought we were going to Disneyland every day.

VIEIRA Shane's studio was actually his apartment, and the vocal booth was in the closet—when you closed the door, a light came on. It was a tiny apartment, but it was just like kickin' it at a friend's place. I was happy to just be making music, so I didn't care about the size of the studio.

What memories do you have surrounding your first single, "Rebirth of Slick (Cool Like Dat)"?

VIEIRA One of Ish's friends had used that Art Blakey sample ["Stretching"] on another song, so out of respect he asked that friend if he could use it—and then he flipped it in a completely different way. It was super tight. Working together was always smooth and easy. We just had this special connection. We liked the same kind of sounds, vibes, and energy. That was my first experience with that kind of magic. We didn't have a lot of money, so sometimes we split a pizza three ways just to eat, but those guys were my family.

IRVING When our manager handed us the cassette single, I just stood there staring at it. Like, *Wow, I finally have a real record.* A few minutes later I was walking down the street and I saw Q-Tip on the other side and I ran over to say hi. I didn't know him at the time, but I was fan. I gave him props, shook his hand, and showed him the Digable single. I was so happy.

BUTLER We had gone to Europe on a promotional tour and by the time we got back to the States, the record had blown up, and video channels were playing the clip over and over. It was a good feeling.

"Cool Like Dat" Went on to win a Grammy in 1994 for Best Rap Performance by a Duo or a Group, beating out Arrested Development, Cypress Hill, Dr. Dre and Snoop Dogg, and Naughty By Nature. Where you surprised when you won?

IRVING Personally, I thought Snoop and Dre were going to win. When they called our names, it was like time stood still. It was mad surreal.

VIEIRA It was a bittersweet night for me, because my mom was very close to passing away; I was grateful that we got to perform with [legendary jazz trumpeter] Clark Terry, but my head and my heart were with her. After that, we went back into the studio to start working on *Blowout Comb*, but whenever we weren't in the studio, I was back with my mother.

Although Blowout Comb was a critical success, it didn't match the first album in terms of sales. However, it's considered a slept-on classic today.

BUTLER "Slept on" always has the notion that it's good, otherwise nobody would care; it's like the music has a nice second existence. Sonically and lyrically, it was a step away from the first album, which was intentional. When Light in the Attic Records approached us about doing reissues

of our music [in 2013], they wanted to release *Blowout Comb* first. So yeah, it was slept on, but I'm cool with that.

Not long after Blowout Comb was released, Pendulum Records folded, and Digable Planets broke up. What happened?

IRVING We're just human beings and we go through things: emotions, stress, ups and downs. We were also young and immature and dealing with certain things in life. There were obstacles because of the music industry, and we didn't know how to handle it. But, at this stage in our lives, we have kids and responsibilities; back then, we were just wild. I don't regret anything that happened, but I'm glad we could get over it and get back together and do things.

BUTLER When we split up, it was more about changing directions in life and creativity rather than about having problems with each other. I was taken aback by the response to us getting back together. The friendship is still there, so whatever obstacles we had are easy to jump over. ✐

103

MICHAEL A. GONZALES *is a Brooklyn-based writer.*

Looking to capitalize on the electronica explosion of the mid-'90s, the American music industry tried to get a number of dance music festivals off the ground—with generally disastrous results.

By Michaelangelo Matos

Crashing Out on the Electric Highway

The spring of 1997 was a make-or-break time for electronic dance music in America. In the midst of an overall sales dip, the U.S. record business was looking for the next big thing, so when a number of dance acts—the Prodigy, Daft Punk, Underworld—cracked the playlists of influential modern rock radio stations, and the Chemical Brothers' second album, *Dig Your Own Hole*, debuted at No. 14 on the Billboard 200 that April, it sent a pink-noise wave through the industry: *This might be it.*

What the American music industry understood (songs) was miles away from what the dance scene that had sired those acts was after (tracks that DJs could segue into one another). But with their hip-hop-derived breakbeats and arena rock dynamics, many of these newer acts could safely slot between Beck and Korn. And just to differentiate this new beat-driven stuff from house music (too gay and urban), or techno and rave (neither had caught on when labels tried selling them in '92), a new name arose as a convenient umbrella for a curious nation: electronica. It was, you know, the "new alt-rock."

That meant concerts, not raves. The previous year, the Chemical Brothers had headlined Organic '96, an outdoor gathering in the San Fernando Valley that specifically emphasized acts that played keyboards and wrangled gear, not DJs. Based on Organic, which drew around 6300 paid attendees, the Chems' booking agent, Gerry Gerrard, attempted to stage a touring festival—redubbed Chaotica—with the Prodigy as the headliner, even going so far as to schedule a '97 date at Madison Square Garden. But Chaotica never got off the ground: The Prodigy wouldn't commit, nor would Organic alums Orbital and the Orb. All three had decided to join that year's alt-rock package-tour warhorse Lollapalooza, along with Korn, Tool, Snoop Dogg, and Damian and Julian Marley. The bill had zero cohesion; Korn dropped off midway into the tour, which wouldn't be staged again for six years. With Gerrard spiking Chaotica, the summer and fall of '97 became open season on electronica tours.

———

Electronica's ascent within the pop world was just the opportunity that Marci Weber, cofounder of MCT Management, was looking for to make her prize client, Moby, a star. She had worked to turn the diminutive DJ/producer—who scored a Top 10 UK hit in 1991 with "Go" and signed with Elektra in 1993—and his highly energetic, largely pre-taped live show into dance music's top draw for a few years, but by mid-decade, there was a sharp disconnect between Moby and the rest of the dance world. He wanted to maintain the frenzy of the early '90s, while the scene grew darker and more serious. His 1995 album *Everything Is Wrong* was a frequently striking and wholly ambitious attempt to prove himself a master of all musical styles, but while rock writers showered it with praise, the hardcore dance press moved on.

He followed the album with *Animal Rights*—issued in England in September 1996, and America in February 1997—which was divisive in every way possible: a snarling rock album nobody was expecting,

ELECTRIC HIGHWAY, 1997
COURTESY OF RAMY, LIVINGART.COM

or wanted, including his management and his fans. Elektra wasn't especially happy either; he was off the label by the end of the year.

"It was funny that I put out an album that was very guitar oriented, and I was ridiculed and ostracized for it, and the Chemical Brothers and Prodigy started using guitars and were celebrated as visionaries," says Moby. "Change is celebrated as long as it's not radical change."

But even after that setback, the possibilities presented by Organic '96 had raised Weber's competitive side: "Part of me was like, 'That's great—it'll open doors for everybody else.' And the other part of me is going, 'Wait a minute—we should've been doing that.'" So Weber set

out to put on a dance-music package tour of her own. Her first pitch was to William Morris, the agency that owned Lollapalooza. Morris signed on. "We were all in shock, and totally excited," says Sheneza Mohammed, who ran Bold Marketing, an MCT arm.

Big Top U.S.A., as Weber dubbed her tour, was only one of the road shows aimed at the raver market that season. There were a couple of others: Electric Highway, sponsored by *SPIN* and BF Goodrich tires; and Moonshine Over America, starring a rotating group of DJs from the roster of L.A. dance label Moonshine Music. Weber remained sanguine about the competition: "I didn't see any of it as a threat because I thought it was a big enough [market]."

"Change is celebrated as long as it's not radical change."

—MOBY

Big Top took two months to put together and showcased most of the major electronic dance trends of the moment. From DJs Grooverider and the No U-Turn Records trio of Ed Rush, Nico, and Trace, who played eerie drum'n'bass, all the way to Weber's burgeoning new American trance star BT, a composer/producer (and adamantly not a DJ) who wrote shamelessly upbeat epics. Twelvetrees, meanwhile, were the management company's "baby act," according to Mohammed. One song title said it all: "The Chillin' Fields."

A brace of Big Top acts—Infected Mushroom, Medicine Drum, Eat Static, Empirion, and Michael Dog—played music that took drum machine abuse to new levels of cosmic abandon—less sky-arcing and melodic, more of a crusty hippie freak-out. The style came to be known as one of the most dire verbal concoctions in dance music's endless subgenre cosmos: psy-trance, which had caught on in New York's East Village. "It was a pretty big scene [there]," says Mohammed

Even for dance music, though, the style was insular—when Mohammed later worked with psy-trance staples Shpongle, she says, "We left the marketing up to them; they knew how to reach their folks. Psy-trance was not going to get played on any radio station."

Making regular pit stops to DJ at Big Top shows were revered Detroit techno pioneers Juan Atkins, Derrick May, and Kevin Saunderson. "I thought it was important not to pass them by," says Weber. "As well as the fact that they're goddamn legends, they're masters of their craft." Today, not one of them recalls anything about the tour. Others with clearer recollections might wish they could say the same.

Electric Highway was put together in much the same way as Big Top. "Richard Bishop managed the Crystal Method and put that tour together to make them stars," recalls Mohammed with a laugh. "All of it was management driven."

"The venues were very awkward—really off-the-wall and far away," says L.A. DJ Doc Martin, who played Electric Highway. "In Salt Lake City, we did it at a huge venue outside the city, by the salt beds." Owing to its tire sponsorship, several dates were at raceways. A number of dance diehards were incensed at this incursion. "I thought the world was ending," says DJ/producer Tommie Sunshine, laughing; he'd gone to Electric Highway's Atlanta date at House of Blues with the words "FUCK CORPORATE RAVE" written across his forehead (given additional space by his then-annual habit of shaving his eyebrows). "I was always fine with this music being commercial as long as it's done the right way," he explains. "But that tour rubbed me the wrong way. They thought they could just step in, and that's not how this works."

Organic '96 organizer Gerry Gerrard had been right: no headliner, no crowd. When journalist David Prince saw Electric Highway at Chicago's Navy Pier on September 5, he recalls, "It was nothing. Nobody was there." Chicago promoter Charles Little II's company Pure worked on that gig with the city's entrenched concert powerhouse, Jam Productions, and tried to show them footage of successful English dance festivals like Creamfields and Tribal Gathering—which the Jam folks ignored. "We were always coming around the corner like, 'No, that's not how it's done,'" says Little. But his stay-underground mindset was hard to shake off: "Jam were the pathway to [our] going from being some kids on the sides to maybe owning an annual, sponsorable, marketable, merchandisable festival. But we weren't even thinking about that."

On September 6 in Minneapolis, Electric Highway's location had to be moved from a horse track to Ground Zero, a nightclub with a capacity of about 600. "It had a chain-link fence separating the DJ booth from the floor," says Doc Martin. A member of MW-Raves, an early dance-music mailing list that preceded the World Wide Web, happened to work at the liquor store across the street from the venue and posted to the list that she'd gotten complimentary tickets from "two guys with BF Goodrich [who] came in and purchased almost $800 worth of water, alcohol, and soda." She was unimpressed: Electric Highway's staging was for a rock concert, not a rave. "I guess I expected too much from a bunch of guys who change tires for a living," she posted.

At least Electric Highway didn't have a headliner who was clearly unhappy to be there. "Going into it, I knew they were going to have a really hard time trying to sell tickets, especially because they booked it into larger venues," says Moby. On August 29, The Big Top stopped at Cleveland's Nautica Park and drew fewer than 500 people; there, Moby grew tetchy at a number of technical snafus that forced him to repeatedly cut off the show. He wasn't alone: Two nights later, the co-promoter in Asbury Park, New Jersey, Concerts East, shut down the event without informing MCT. On September 9, in Dallas, Big Top went so far into the red that Moby returned his fee just to make sure the crew got paid; that same night in Seattle, Derrick May played a non-tour date at the downtown club Re-bar, where a fan mentioned a forthcoming Big Top San Francisco date that May was scheduled to play. "Don't go!" he responded. "It's going to suck!"

The tour's morale was flagging, but everybody figured it would be better once they hit California. Big Top was set to played the Bay Area on September 12 and L.A.'s Snow Valley next day. (Electric Highway played the same cities, in reverse, on those same two dates.) But the S.F. show got moved to the Oakland International Event Center, with three huge rooms. "We thought everything was fine," says Weber. "We were going to have a really fantastic sound system and open, raw warehouse space that nobody was going to bother [us] in. This is the way it's supposed to be; this is how they do it in England." The kids could get there with little trouble, too—the venue was a short walk from a Bay Area Rapid Transit station.

There was a problem, though: The BART had gone on strike five days before Big Top's arrival. One member of the SF-Raves mailing list reported a five-hour journey via "tram, bus, train, and boat, instead of BART." Another partygoer resorted to a Greyhound from San Francisco to Oakland. "We felt so bad," says Weber. "What else could happen? Is this a black cloud? Half the people couldn't get there. We were supposed to do really well at that show."

The doors opened at 5 p.m., and crowds were sparse for hours: One partygoer compared it to "entering the Death Star." The crowd swelled in size around midnight, but even at its peak, the audience was swallowed by the venue. "Most people there [were] either selling drugs or... checking out the scene for the first time," one SF-Raver posted; another was aghast that "no one was dancing!"

Nor did it help that the billing order was completely haphazard, with DJs alternating with live acts, whether or not the transitions made sense. Hence drum'n'bass segued awkwardly into 808 State in rock-band mode, while Joey Beltram's hard techno and a four-turntable dual-DJ round by Atkins and May sandwiched Headrillaz—a crew of Brits trying their damnedest to be the Prodigy with rapping. Often, the DJs' sets were drowned out by the sound of the bands behind them doing their soundcheck. "A band would finish their set, and 10 minutes later a DJ would start, while in the meantime everyone would leave to go to another room, and the whole thing just didn't flow," an SF-Raver posted.

In Oakland, the crowd complained about the way the dance scene had changed, as well as the evening's ticket prices, which topped out at $30, after years of large parties costing under $20. About halfway through the night, the main room's soundman told Weber, "I'm cutting the sound and lights. I haven't been paid." Weber had to strong-arm her partners to pony up: "It was all or nothing." A half hour later, the police showed up to check things out—an officer later told one partygoer that 17 cars were broken into that night. "Just one nightmare after the next," says Weber.

By 3 a.m., the venue was mostly empty again. Shortly afterward, Atkins and May began their tag-team set. Two hours later, May stepped away from the decks and began chatting with some of the throng when he spotted his Seattle fan, stopped mid-sentence, and crowed: "I told you it was going to suck!"

The following day in L.A., MCT partnered with Insomniac, the city's largest dance promoters, run by Pasquale Rotella and Philip Blaine, who absorbed the lineup into their annual blowout, Nocturnal Wonderland. Rotella told them, "You might have all these big names, but that's not why people are going." Insomniac still did everything big and outlandish, as if 1992 hadn't ended. "When we worked with Nocturnal Wonderland, it was this massive, tri-folded flyer, and they used their classic hippie-dippy enchanted-forest stuff," says Mohammed. "In that market, that's what the kids expected. They set up everything from sumo wrestling to a Ferris wheel." Nocturnal Wonderland 1997 drew 5,500; the next day, Electric Highway drew a mere one-tenth of Big Top's crowd.

But it still wasn't enough to push Big Top out of the red.

———

Big Top lost its shirt because it didn't have a sponsor. Moonshine Over America (MOA) took no such chances. Camel cigarettes was ramping up its presence in American nightclubs, providing branded napkins, sponsoring event nights, and even backing a late-'90s DJ-centric magazine called *Sweater*. Moonshine founder Steve Levy mapped the route with Paul Morris, who had recently opened AM Only, a DJ booking agency, taking an office in the back of Manhattan's all-drum'n'bass shop Breakbeat Science. Their tour started when Big Top and Electric Highway ended, on purpose: "We didn't want to run against them over the summer," says Levy.

It wasn't MOA's only piece of strategy. Unlike Big Top and Electric Highway, Levy made sure to include his tour stops' local promoters from the ground up. They also carefully mapped out who'd play where—if a DJ had played a city less than six months earlier, they sat out.

The exception was Superstar DJ Keoki, the New Yorker who'd come to fame as a resident at the notorious Limelight, playing parties for promoter and one-time boyfriend Michael Alig. "Keoki was getting booked a little earlier around the country than any other U.S. DJ," says Levy. Following notorious "Geraldo" and "Donahue" appearances, Alig's extravagant crew of partygoing friends, dubbed the Club Kids, began making pilgrimages to other U.S. cities, where local promoters, like Cleveland's Rob Sherwood, would hire them for the weekend: "We'd book their plane and [give them] a dozen tickets."

Keoki brought that same reckless impulsiveness to MOA. "He was legendary for partying like a rock star," says Levy. "His thing was missing flights." The first MOA was done entirely by plane; Levy likens gathering DJs at airports en masse to "herding cats." In Toronto, Keoki "went through customs, straight from the show, in leopard-skin pants with his shirt off, a bandolier around him."

"On the Seattle leg the second year—the first time we had the bus—he showed up with leather shorts, a knitted tank top, roller skates, and a Viking helmet," says Moonshine DJ John Kelley. "He was passing balloons out." Another time, Kelley recalls, "There was some trouble—he'd trashed a hotel room or something. To make it up to everybody, he made us peanut butter and jelly sandwiches when he rejoined the tour."

Neither Big Top nor Electric Highway ever went on the road again, but Moonshine Over America would go out for three more years. The inaugural Moonshine tour came to an end on October 24, 1997, in New Orleans, the city where, three years later, a federal crackdown would begin that would put a halt to the U.S. rave scene for most of the 2000s. A week later, Keoki's ex-boyfriend Michael Alig was sentenced 10 to 20 years in prison for manslaughter.

The party was over. ✐

111

———

MICHAELANGELO MATOS *is a music journalist who recently published* The Underground is Massive: How Electronic Dance Music Conquered America.

FYF MUSIC FESTIVAL, 2013
PHOTO BY JONATHAN LEIBSON/WIREIMAGE

Welcome to the Beach House Sensory Deprivation Extravaganza!

By Jillian Mapes

Around the time Alex Scally started Beach House with Victoria Legrand in 2004, the guitarist and keyboardist was working alongside his father as a carpenter in Baltimore.

That training has served him well in one of indie rock's most tireless touring bands, the sort of act that does more than a hundred dates across three or four continents with every album: Scally has hand built many of Beach House's live set-pieces.

Over the last decade, their onstage design has moved beyond the scope of carpentry—toward sheets of organza hanging amid layered light on their current tour behind last year's *Depression Cherry* and *Thank Your Lucky Stars*—but Scally and Legrand still design their own shows. This is rarer than one might think for an act of their level, but it's not exactly surprising: Beach House's music chases the ever-nebulous "vibe," but it's meticulous in capturing the vibe imagined. Beach House's shows, by extension, attempt to offer a visual manifestation of the duo's dreamy soundscapes with a strategic use of light; they'll carve little patterns of it and start layering, they'll remove it completely, they'll shroud themselves in deep blues and reds as the songs call for it. Of course, all this subtle mood-building is infinitely easier to do in a dark club before a couple of thousand people than at a big outdoor festival. Nevertheless, festivals are part of the game, so Beach House play those, too.

By the time the summer comes to a close, Beach House will have played—as a four-piece with bassist/keyboardist Skyler Skjelset and drummer James Barone—Coachella, both Primavera Sounds, Outside Lands, Pickathon, FYF, Hopscotch, Best Kept Secret in the Netherlands, and Pitchfork Music Festival in Chicago, where they'll headline. Before they really got into the swing of things on the fest front, we spoke with Scally by phone from Baltimore about the challenges that accompany main-stage territory, the band's most miserable festival appearances, and how great Guns N' Roses (supposedly) were at this year's Coachella.

113

FYF MUSIC FESTIVAL, 2013

PHOTO BY CHELSEA LAUREN/WIREIMAGE

BEACH HOUSE

TPR   **You and Victoria are meticulous about setting a palpable, often dark mood with your club shows, but then you play so many festivals. How do you translate that into big outdoor stages?**

AS   Tour is a constantly evolving thing. It took us, like, 50 shows to get the show where it's at now, so that's why, for festivals, we're trying to just do the exact same thing. We spent two or three days trying to figure out how to make an outdoor festival feel as much like our show as possible. Our show is based a lot on projections—using projectors as if they were light fixtures—so we found different projectors that are high-powered for outdoors and set them up in different angles. It's all about dimensions, contrast, patterns, motion, lots of negative space.

We use a fabric [organza] for our regular show [as the backdrop] that we've really fallen in love with, because it really appears and disappears, but it's not equipped for wind or even the outdoors, and neither is the rigging. So we ordered this different fabric [textilene, like a PVC-coated polyester] that's made for high wind, and we demoed it. We were able to use it at the first Coachella, but not the second one because there was a windstorm.

It was a little different, but we were able to use all of the same cues and equipment, more or less. We felt good that it did feel like our show, but we'll learn a lot as we go on.

Has this trial and error of alternate materials and stagings has gotten easier over time?
We've been doing this so much, for so long, that things have grown simpler as time's gone on. We've also learned what to fight for, and to not worry too much. We've gotten way more like, "Something's broken, let's just play music as much as we can and if people like it, they'll like it."

With the rise of electronic music, festivals can almost be too dependent on visual aspects. Not to be one of those old-timers, but I kind of love when I see shows where [the performers are] like, "Let's just play music up here." I'm not a huge Guns N' Roses fan at all, and I actually didn't really know much about them, but I saw them at Coachella—the second weekend, apparently the first weekend they were terrible—and I was super into how they had nothing going on, really. A couple of lights. But I was like, "Damn, these guys just played some rock music for two and a half hours up there." That was cool.

Is putting together a setlist for a festival differently than planning one for your own show?
We definitely alter the set a little bit and make it more energetic—as much as we do "energetic." But we still try to write a little story. We don't just want [the setlist] to be non sequitur. We don't write setlists ahead of time, though. One of the things we do every day on tour is wait to see what's happening in each place. What's the energy like here? What are the people like? What's the venue like? Are we in a tent or on a stage? All of that information factors heavily into what we decide to play on a given day.

It was really strange playing Coachella, because every other thing happening around us was hard EDM. Flume was after us. Diplo was before us. Calvin Harris was the headliner that night. It was all this intense, super loud music. Our show relies quite heavily on sensory deprivation: One of the things we always try to do is get people to expect less as soon as they walk in—have it be really dark, really quiet. As we create music, the more subtle things emerge. But at Coachella, people were just getting blasted so hard all day, by the time they came

to us, it was like we weren't even there. The sound just couldn't compete with the sensory destruction they had been undergoing the entire day.

It's really crazy how different all festivals really are. Primavera is a late festival, and it's really moody, wonderful, kind of romantic. There's a lot more liberties there. You don't have to feel [the responsibility to be] as entertaining—people will go with you on more of a journey.

Do you remember the very first festival you played?
It was the 2007 Pitchfork Festival, which was a total disaster. We so weren't prepared for what was expected. We were on a side stage and there was a loud band playing—we couldn't hear ourselves at all. We weren't used to the whole thing of, "You have 20 minutes to get onstage and get everything together." I think it was a pretty poor performance. We were still sitting down at that point. We learned a lot in those early years.

Any other disastrous festival performances that taught you something?
Before we had sound people, we wrote a song called

SALA APOLO, 2015
PHOTO BY XAVI TORRENT/REDFERNS

"We usually don't accept a festival unless we can play at night. Daytime really doesn't work for us."

Alex Scally

"Festival." It was like a three-minute song that we thought sounded cool, where each instrument came in one at a time. It was designed so that every time an instrument came in, we could look over to the monitor person and say "up" or "down," so that those first three minutes of the show weren't a disaster. That was a big thing we did for about a year, around 2009. But we had a really, really bad show at Sasquatch in 2009—probably one of the worst shows of our entire career.

What happened?
Literally just screeching feedback for 25 minutes. Like, you're playing a song but it's not a song and nothing's happening. You're confused. The audience is confused. People are walking away.

You're not screeching feedback now, but do you still see any of the audience casually come and go at festivals? And does it bother you at all?
You can't be a baby and complain about that. You said yes to the festival, you have to expect that someone's going to walk up and be like, "This band sucks!" and walk away. Festivals can be really amazing, but I also think that they're not the best thing for listeners. They're like the Costco of music experiences: You get more for less money, but it's always of a lower quality. The bands don't sound check, and the crowd is in a weird, uncomfortable situation. Sometimes they can be insanely magical, but also sometimes they can be kind of a sad affair, where nothing sounds that great, or looks that great, or is that great. Everybody's struggling. It's also sometimes the cooler, early-day bands that suffer the most, because they're not prepared for that situation. They just aren't experienced or don't have a lot of crew; sometimes you really lose out at festivals in that position.

At this point, Beach House will always play at night on a festival lineup, right?
We usually don't accept a festival unless we can play at night, just because we think that's where our music makes the most sense. We've begged and asked for it— daytime really doesn't work for us. ✍

117

JILLIAN MAPES *is an editor at Pitchfork. She lives in New York.*

THE
ART
OF
RAVE

BY MARC HOGAN

POSTERS COURTESY OF MATTHEW JOHNSON

ON
JULY 3
1993

Matthew Johnson was one of thousands dancing at the second installment of Let Freedom Rave, a massive outdoor party series thrown by a group of San Francisco promoters known as the Gathering. On this holiday eve, the venue was a dirt motorbike track in the East Bay, where summers are typically too tinderbox-dry for Fourth of July fireworks. But someone tossed a bottle rocket anyway, with predictably incendiary results.

As Johnson, now 44, recalls, most people initially mistook a burning tree for one of the party's visual effects. "Everybody was super excited about it, jumping up and down," he says. The mood changed when a fire marshal arrived to shut down the party, but rather than let the night come to an early end, a crew of ravers charged the blaze with water and eventually extinguished the flames. "The music started up again—it was like a reboot," Johnson remembers fondly. "That was a really good time."

That rescued blowout is one of the tens of thousands archived in the Rave Preservation Project, an exhaustive online database of underground dance memorabilia that Johnson has lovingly compiled over the last three years. A veteran and sometime DJ in the underground Bay Area electronic music scene, Johnson started the Rave Preservation Project in May 2013 out of a desire to share his own personal trove of flyers—what was then about 1000 items—with friends who'd been there too. Before long, rave collectors from around the world were sending in their own souveneirs.

Now the Rave Preservation Project hosts flyers from at least 17 countries and 33 U.S. states, though the overwhelming focus is on Johnson's native California, an early American hotbed for the movement. Despite the geographical separation, one common aesthetic theme is a sense of neon joy not too far removed from utopian Woodstock ideals. Regional differences do emerge: In California, two-tone flyers oriented around simple graphic design principles were the initial norm, evolving by the mid-1990s into busier, more colorful, text-filled approaches. European rave flyers, by comparison, were more art driven, tending to use scans or photos of actual paintings. The oldest materials on Johnson's site, like San Diego's Playskool parties, date back to the mid-1980s and applied a do-it-yourself resourcefulness that involved crude drawings or magazine photocopies.

121

Johnson, a self-described entrepreneur who recently launched a mobile photo-organization app called Odibly, doesn't consider himself a collector, but a kind of cultural archivist. "I'm not doing this for myself," he says. It's clearly a labor of love: In a week, he'll spend anywhere from 10 to 40 hours updating the database. "I'm doing it for the community."

TOONTOWN
the Ultimate Session

FEATURING LIVE
TEN CITY
INTERNATIONAL DJ JAM
on six turntables with live keyboards
SATURDAY SEPTEMBER 5th 1992

SAN FRANCISCO 1992

TPR **Tell me about your first rave.**

MJ   When this whole thing started—warehouse parties, break-in parties with basic lights—they were called "undergrounds." It really wasn't until things went mainstream that people started calling them raves. And raves were a little different, because there was a lot more money put into them: Big promoters came in, started getting bouncy castles, and all that crazy stuff.

My first underground was in the late '80s. Some friends of mine who were older—they were going to UC Davis and I was still in high school—wanted to go to a political rally in Sacramento. Afterward, there was this warehouse party going on, so we drove past it and you heard the bass. Inside, in this tiny little warehouse, there were maybe a couple of hundred people, a strobe light, a black light, a smoke machine, and a DJ booth set up in the corner—and that was it. People were dancing, having a good time; there was no ego, no drama. For me, it was perfect. I danced all night—I didn't do any drugs—but I almost immediately fell in love with it. That's how I got involved with that scene.

How did you start collecting flyers?

By accident, really. I'm not a collector; I don't collect things. But I was always into the underground scene. When I was a kid, I was into punk rock and had a bunch of memorabilia because I used to flyer for punk shows in the Sacramento area—but I ended up losing it all. I was too young to be there in the 1970s when punk really started, so when the whole electronic music underground began and I was part of that, I held onto a box of flyers from the late '80s, early '90s, from mostly San Francisco and the Bay Area. Eventually, I decided to scan the stuff—about 1000 pieces from 1000 events, which took forever—and built a super basic website and sent it to some friends. All of a sudden, people started sending me their old flyers and it built itself organically.

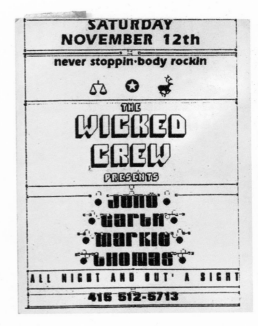

SAN FRANCISCO *Year Unknown*

123

What's the importance of archiving these?

Personal value is one reason. There're a lot of memories. I was there—and a lot of my friends were there—in the beginning of what became this huge mainstream movement, from the drugs and the music to the fashion. Showing the younger generation, in a visual way, where the stuff they've taken on as their identities started—that was important to preserve. My turntables are older than the kids who go out these days! So there's no way they could know what it was like when the whole thing started. But I do.

Also, the collection brings inspiration: I get emails from graphic designers and artists who look through the website for ideas.

PLAYSKOOL
GRAND OPENING
OCTOBER 10th
AT THE HOTEL SAN
DIEGO ON BROADWAY

1 years gets in
21 years gets alcohol drin
I.D. REQUIRED
open from 9-2 a.
ALL AGES ONE L
PRICE: $5.00

HOTEL SAN DIEGo

APRIL 24

FRIDAY NOV. 14
at the 'Hotel San Die
corner of Broadway and

...NIGHT CL

PLAYSKOOL IS BA

COME*UNITY

MUSIC

1015 FOLSOM @ 6th

Mixed By:
Ernie
Garth
Jerry

MARCH 5th '91

GLO

CITRUSONIC
DDEN FRUIT

SATURDA
SEPTEMBE

YELLOW

DOUBLE
DIPPED
PROD
SENDS
YOU
TO
THE
YEAR
40,000

Tri-

TAKEN ON

AS THEIR

IDENTITIES

SAN FRANCISCO *Year Unknown*

Where did the rave flyer aesthetic come from?

In the beginning, there really wasn't money involved [with these parties]: Somebody had sounds, somebody had records, somebody had a black light and a strobe light, so a lot of the design was drawing something or cutting a picture out of a magazine, then running to Kinko's and firing off copies.

And back then, most of the undergrounds were promoted by word of mouth or phone trees, so there really wasn't a need for flyers: When [organizers] released the location, one person would call 10 people, those 10 would call 10 more people, those 100 would call 10 others—and that's how the word would get out.

But even when there were flyers, the graphic art was super basic and primitive. The early [Let Freedom Rave] parties, for example, didn't have a location on the flyer; they'd have a phone number. You would call a number, and it would say, "Call this number back at the night of the event," usually somewhere around 11 p.m. The night of the event, you would call at 11 p.m., and there would be a voice recording of a map-point location. So you would go to that point and different things would happen: It might be that they would send you to another place, to screen who is showing up—so that if cops or somebody who looked super sketchy were trying to go, they'd just ignore them.

Or there was a map point at a gas station. You'd park around the corner, walk over, and there'd be somebody who would tell you to go into a house, where they would then give you a little piece of paper with directions. It wouldn't have a name of the event, it wouldn't have any DJs or phone numbers—nothing—so if you dropped it on the street, there wouldn't be any information except where you're going.

Later on, as events started to be thrown by promoters who were going to charge, they would have more money to put into big, bright, colorful flyers. But in the beginning, it was really cheap, it was really underground, and it wasn't about making money.

What legendary rave locations do you have flyers for?

Bonny Doon is a beach between San Francisco and Santa Cruz. Back before the cops really knew what this was all about, a lot of after-parties and a lot of full-moon parties would end up there. To get there, you'd drive along the Pacific Coast Highway to the dunes and you'd park. You walk down this huge sand ramp until you get to this private cove surrounded by cliffs. The only thing out there is farms, so there's not really people and you'd just have the sound of the waves. People would bring cardboard to dance on, because you can't really dance on sand. It was this amazing place.

What's the legacy of raves in today's world of music festivals like Electric Daisy Carnival?

That's a tough one. The whole underground movement paved the way for big festivals. But when you have an underground movement, it's people trying to do something different, usually with a set of ideals—but it's really a movement to be an individual and to be yourself. Now the big music festivals are more for promoters as a business to make money. And then people jump on, like lemmings.

I personally don't like big festivals. I never have. I don't even like big concerts. ✑

MARC HOGAN *is based in Iowa and is a senior staff writer at Pitchfork.*

SAN FRANCISCO *1992*

A Tribute to the Eternal Teenage Symphony

By Ron Hart

Illustrations by Jacob Stead

This year, Brian Wilson is celebrating the Beach Boys' *Pet Sounds* by taking the 1966 masterpiece around the world on tour one last time, including a stop at Chicago's Pitchfork Festival. In honor of the album's 50th anniversary, we enlisted artists from across the musical spectrum—including members of Talking Heads, Yo La Tengo, Chairlift, and Deftones—to look back on its infinite influence.

If ever there were an artist so perfectly able to tap into the creativity of his inner child, it is Brian Wilson. In the time leading up to the May 16, 1966 release of the Beach Boys' *Pet Sounds*, Wilson—who was only in his early twenties—erupted with a manic wellspring of ideas, visions, and fleeting thoughts.

The songwriter suffered a panic attack while on a flight from Los Angeles to Houston two days before Christmas in 1964, which prompted him to stop touring with his band altogether. Then came the 1965 hit "California Girls," which reportedly marked the first time Wilson composed a song while under the influence of psychedelics. He took in the Beatles' then-brand-new album *Rubber Soul*, which challenged him to rethink his entire method of music-making. With an opus in his brain, he headed to the studio. Compelled to break out of the surfing-boy-band box the Beach Boys were locked inside, Wilson sat out of the group's tour of Japan in January 1966 to create the 36-minute pocket symphony that would shatter every preconceived notion the world had about the band—and even popular music itself.

Considering Wilson's lack of formal training in arrangement and composition, the way he translated his ideas to the album's orchestral format is nothing short of magic. Though he was awed by Phil Spector's production on the Ronettes' 1963 hit "Be My Baby," with *Pet Sounds*, Wilson didn't construct a Wall of Sound as much as a sonic sandbox. (Later on, he would have an actual sandbox built in his mansion while he created the Beach Boys' intended follow-up, *SMiLE*.) And while *Pet Sounds* did yield its fair share of individual hits, the record was meant to be heard as a themed song cycle. At its root, the album is a story that takes you along the complete arc of emotions that coincide with falling in love with someone—from hope to elation to worry to despair—a far cry from the steady diet of songs about girls, cars, and surfing that had been the band's primary M.O. since their formation in 1961.

Pet Sounds has cast an impossibly wide net these last 50 years, informing the worlds of rock, hip-hop, jazz, electronic, experimental, punk, pop, and just about everything else you can imagine. The wide swath of artists assembled for this feature represents a modicum of the album's vast influence. Its scope transcends age, race, and gender, and its impact continues to broaden with each passing generation.

133

Sean Ono Lennon

I'm embarrassed to say that—perhaps due to a lack of sophistication on my part, or the misheard echoes of a supposed rivalry between my father's group and the Beach Boys—I was late to understand the music of Brian Wilson. It wasn't until after puberty, after discovering Hendrix, after listening to Miles Davis, and after my own feeble attempts at songwriting, that my ears opened up and I suddenly found my universe transformed by *Pet Sounds*.

I was 21 years old and had just about finished recording my first album, *Into the Sun*, at Sear Sound in New York. At the time, my only professional gig had been playing bass in Cibo Matto, and I was playing some of my tracks for their manager, and I remember him saying, "This kind of sounds like a Brian Wilson record." Slightly offended, I replied cynically: "Surf music?" After some quiet gasping, I believe it was the engineer Tom Schick who told me to be quiet. And suddenly I found myself listening to "God Only Knows."

Brian once described how drinking water after his first hash joint felt like his "first glass of water," and I felt the same way when listening to "God Only Knows" at that moment. This was the first time I'd ever heard a song. It was the beginning of my true musical education. No longer would I be self-taught; from now on I would be attending a graduate course at the Brian Wilson School of Music.

I ravenously consumed each song on the album, overcome by a sort of madness. I couldn't stop listening to "God Only Knows" until I knew every single note of every instrument and vocal. I'd never played a major 6 or a minor major 7; I'd heard those colors before, but *Pet Sounds* made me see them and desire them, and to this day I hunger for them: for the intricacies of counterpoint, of suspending chords by avoiding the root note on the bass, and for the interlocking molecular geometry of well-composed harmonies. Brian Wilson is my Bach.

I could've learned these things from the Beatles, perhaps, but that music was so primordial and fundamental to me—it had always been there, like the sun or the moon. Of course, after I returned to *Revolver* and *Sgt. Pepper's* armed with the X-ray goggles I'd been given while making my way through *Pet Sounds*, I suddenly heard that

music for the first time as well. I can't imagine a greater gift. Nothing has ever made me feel more connected to the universe and ultimately to the work of my father. For this, I have Mr. Wilson to thank.

Air's Jean-Benoît Dunckel

In French, "pet" doesn't mean an animal, it means "fart." So when I first read this album's title, I thought it was really funny. Then I noticed that the music sounded much more harmonious than the kind of sounds that the French word referred to; I don't know any other pop album that's as sophisticated as *Pet Sounds*.

Yo La Tengo's Ira Kaplan

I didn't really like *Pet Sounds* when I first heard it. I was reading a lot about music at the time, so I knew I was getting to hear this legendary record. But I didn't get it at first. It's a very subtle record. But I just kept listening. And then one night I pulled it out and all the tumblers clicked into place and my appreciation for it was unlocked.

Matmos' Drew Daniel

Everybody loves *Pet Sounds*. It is one of those records that is not just about its sounds and songs but also the total set of meanings we have attached to it as we listen, play and replay it, cover it, customize it, sling it onto mixtapes and playlists, and embroider it with experiences over time. *Pet Sounds* has scored millions of private movies, intimate encounters, and even more close calls and near misses looked back upon with wistful regret. I have seen more than one student film that used "God Only Knows" as a trampoline on which to bounce back into private memories, and while I'm a sucker for this record like everyone else, I also feel that weird protective thing, thinking, *Don't use it in your art, it's too powerful for that*. It's that kind of canonical album.

We have also learned that the beauty and sweetness of *Pet Sounds* is not as simple as it looks. The gambit of innocence is directly engaged in the cover image, in which we are invited to see adorable-looking animals with soft fur, and adorable-looking Beach Boys with shiny, clean hair as roughly analogous inhabitants of a peaceable, stoned kingdom. But we also know that, given the troubled backstory of Brian Wilson's life, such visions of

innocence are always in dialogue with and threatened by experience, pain, limitations, and negativity—which made the appearance of *Pet Sounds* at a key moment in Patricia Lockwood's long, brilliant poem "Rape Joke" so startling when I read it a few years ago.

As its title makes plain, "Rape Joke" is a harrowing poem about the question of whether we can gain control over trauma through humor, and about whether art is strong enough to provide a framework around shattering moments, and also about the way that abusers and rapists can, horrifically, attempt to close over the facts of their actions with token gestures of care and concern. It was, finally, the artwork strong enough to engage *Pet Sounds*, to incorporate it and not to be overwhelmed by it. Now, for me, the two artworks operate in a force field in which they necessarily include each other; there is no *Pet Sounds* without "Rape Joke" anymore, and no "Rape Joke" without *Pet Sounds*. I am not trying to ruin anyone's favorite album, but I am being honest about the way that art changes over time as later works—when they are strong enough—start to talk back to them. Read it and weep.

Cullen Omori

Of all my favorite "psychedelic" records by '60s juggernauts, *Pet Sounds* probably comes last for me, after the Rolling Stones' *Their Satanic Majesties Request* and *Sgt. Pepper's*. However, I do give *Pet Sounds* kudos for being the first to veer off the boy-band path and dig deep—real, real deep. The album offered a glimpse of how the studio, a place of more constraints than opportunities in the '60s, could be used as an instrument. But the Beach Boys never really resonated with me—though the Brian Wilson movie they just made with John Cusack and the guy with the big schlong from *The Girl Next Door* was all right. I love the story about Brian Wilson pulling over to the side of the road to cry after hearing "Be My Baby" on the radio; I can relate to that story way more than *Pet Sounds*.

Ronnie Spector

I remember seeing Brian at Gold Star Studios when I was recording "Be My Baby"—he was so excited, peeking through the glass. Later, he told me he wrote "Don't Worry Baby" for me as a follow-up to that song. I loved how he arranged harmonies; we both loved the vocal groups of the '50s. I got a chance to sing with Brian when we did my song "I Can Hear Music," and he did this incredible harmony that blew me away—there is no one else who could have come up with that part. The early- to mid-'60s had a more simple approach to life and romance, and that's what I miss about music now. Brian always had an innocence about his music, so pure. That's Brian.

Wild Nothing's Jack Tatum

My parents had a big record collection, but they didn't have any Beach Boys records. My dad was more into stuff like the Byrds and Buffalo Springfield, so in his mind the Beach Boys were just fluff. So I always had that idea in my mind that they weren't worth listening to. And then high school comes around and somebody told me I should

listen to *Pet Sounds*, and I loved it. I immediately went to my dad and said, "Did you even listen to *Pet Sounds*?" He was all like, "Well, yeah, it's OK." There's a certain innocence to the album that is relatable. It's like the first emo record.

Open Mike Eagle

I came to *Pet Sounds* when I used to write an online music column. I had fallen in love with the song "Cherish" by the Association and wrote that it was like a Beach Boys song but that it couldn't be a Beach Boys song because they weren't capable of doing anything that good. You could imagine the barrage of hate mail I got saying that I had obviously not heard *Pet Sounds*—and indeed I hadn't. But then I listened to it and fell all the way in love. I had heard "Caroline, No" years before, when it was covered by They Might Be Giants on their EP *Indestructible Object*. It was my favorite song on that record, and I had no idea it was a cover; I've made numerous beats out of both versions. I had also loved Frank Black's cover of "Hang on to Your Ego" and didn't know that was a cover at the time either. I wrote a song about the financial crisis of 2008 over a beat that sampled "I Know There's an Answer." Having become more familiar with the album and its production, I have heard a lot of those same found-sound techniques used by Timbaland, Dilla, and many more.

Chairlift's Patrick Wimberly

I remember listening to *Pet Sounds* when I was about 7 years old—I assume it had something to do with my childhood love of the song "Kokomo." I think "Kokomo" brought the Beach Boys to a lot of people in my generation—that and their appearance on an episode of "Full House." I liked the album then, but it wasn't until much later that I realized the depth of its artistry.

In 2012, when I married my wife, "God Only Knows" played during our first dance. It was performed by a group of my closest friends and musicians, and it was a beautiful moment in my life. The lyrics in this song are still some of my favorite lyrics ever written. To me, it is not just about falling in love, it is about being endlessly in love.

Talking Heads' Tina Weymouth

When [Talking Heads] were signed to Sire, we were immediately under the wing of Warner Bros., which was the label of the Beach Boys at the time. And it helped us a lot that they were so in love with the Beach Boys, because there were difficulties with Brian Wilson, and his need for great care in regards to his condition—which was being a very sensitive artist—made it so that we were allowed to do what we needed to do as opposed to being pushed into a preconceived mold. I don't think Talking Heads would've had the longevity we did if the label didn't have this wonderful view toward artists. That was the great thing about the music industry back then: There was room for everybody, and a few artists would sell a lot of records to enable those of us who did not sell in quantity to do our thing.

Sunflower Bean's Julia Cumming

I remember walking to school and listening to "I Just Wasn't Made for These Times" over and over again and feeling like, *Oh my god, this song is for me*. It's for every self-deprecating, overly sensitive, emotional kid who

is feeling lonely and just wants to figure it out. I mean, who hasn't been there? In another way, I feel like I wasn't made for these times because I can't figure out how turn on the TV in my own home and I play rock music in 2016.

Daedelus

I'm sure others can speak elegantly about the songcraft and extravagant orchestrations that produced arguably the most auteur album ever recorded. But I'd just focus on the Tannerin, which appears on "I Just Wasn't Made for These Times" (and more prominently on "Good Vibrations"). It's a Theremin-like instrument that was used on sci-fi soundtracks, but completely from outer space in pop music. The vision of Brian Wilson! The gumption, even. It's like he plucked the future from 1966 and invented G-funk and acid house. I'm sure it must have sounded crazy on the radio dial; it certainly did for me.

Car Seat Headrest's Will Toledo

There's never been a perfect Beach Boys album; Brian Wilson was not that consistent of a writer. But *Pet Sounds* is an interesting piece because it's the one that strives the most to achieve this technical perfection, which isn't necessarily my bag. But it made sense for Wilson to do it, because he was trying to blend this high art with pop music—the struggle is to find complex ways to say something that is very simple. "Wouldn't It Be Nice" is built around a very simple chord progression, but all these variations keep getting added in and changing everything. He was trying to figure out how much the general public was willing to accept as far as the complexities of a pop song.

Ezra Furman

When listening to *Pet Sounds*, it's hard to think about anything but the total gorgeousness of the music and all the insanely deep emotions it provokes in me—which is why I never felt comfortable saying it had any influence on me. It's so advanced that I find it rather embarrassing when the average, mostly amateur indie musician claims to be influenced by *Pet Sounds*. Really? It's like the Ramones claiming to be influenced by Bach. I get that you listened to the album and loved it, but come on. You're not operating on anything close to that level.

"The early to mid '60s had a more simple approach to life and romance, and that's what I miss about music now. Brian always had an innocence about his music, so pure." —*Ronnie Spector*

Tacocat's Emily Nokes

I imagined the lyrics on *Pet Sounds* were literal representations of how Brian Wilson felt in real life—he was sometimes in love, sometimes conflicted, sometimes wanted to go home, sometimes whining about Caroline's hair. The subtle panic in his voice and the increasing drum intensity near the end of "I'm Waiting for the Day" felt far more interesting than songs about taking your favorite car to your favorite beach with your favorite girl and your favorite surfboard.

Mogwai's Stuart Braithwaite

Along with *Forever Changes* and *Are You Experienced?*, *Pet Sounds* showed me that the late '60s had been a period when music went on a rapid journey from pop to real invention, and the level of studio imagination is what I've mostly taken from this record. The possibilities displayed through multiple overdubbing were definitely an influence on the way Mogwai record our music, and *Pet Sounds* was one of the first places I heard it done.

Shilpa Ray

Whenever I listened to *Pet Sounds*, I dreamt of my great escape to Southern California, where loss, loneliness, change, and depression could be felt and expressed in Technicolor. I could envision Tommy Morgan's bass harmonica as the warm blasts of the Santa Ana winds, Wilson's organ as the big golden sun, and Carol Kaye's basslines as the playful strut of beautiful beach bunnies dotting the coastline against the vast Pacific Ocean. That said, this is not the SoCal of Black Flag, N.W.A, or Charles Manson. There's no violence here, no gang or race wars, and no one dies in the end. Pets Sounds is the SoCal of a heavy, hazy, medicated '60s love, for when *you feel so broke up, you wanna go home.* At the last fade, when you hear the train leaving, all the ear candy and innocence slowly disappears. Then the dog starts to bark and the anesthetic completely wears off. The movie is over, the dream is over, and it is time again for the browns and greys, the bills and work, the antagonistic exes and shit-covered snow. I know there's no reality without grit, ugliness, or hate, but I still spin *Pet Sounds* from time to time for its gentle, meticulous way of mixing pain with palm trees to help the medicine go down.

Larkin Grimm

It makes me feel all warm and fuzzy just thinking about that music; I can sing the whole album from beginning to end from memory. I love "Caroline, No" in particular, even if it's a little antifeminist: just the idea that a woman could be ruined, that innocence and naivety are the most attractive qualities, that cutting her hair short and getting practical and real and wise would render her unlovable. But I love that song anyway.

PC Worship

It took me years to breach *Pet Sounds*' exhaustive stature and cultural identity and really appreciate it beyond the soundtrack/FM radio monolith it became. I remember finally "getting it" in my friend's Ford Explorer in high school, while we drove around getting high in the suburbs, being taken aback that this music had been sitting in front of us this whole time, that there was this dark unfolding complexity within these short, recognizable pop songs that we had always been exposed to. It really is a strange album.

Talking Heads' Chris Frantz

When I first heard "Sloop John B," I thought it was a Beach Boys song, but it's actually a Bahamian folk song. And one of my friends in the Bahamas said to me, "Oh, the Sloop John B was my grandfather's boat." It was

actually a mail boat that would go across the islands; it's how they get their supplies and so forth. The Sloop John B often didn't work very well, but they could never stop to do maintenance because they were under pressure to deliver the goods. The thing was always breaking down on them. That's where it comes from.

Mr. Lif

Pet Sounds' relevance in my life has actually grown with time, because the themes Wilson touches upon are so heartfelt and real that one inevitably finds a route to his wisdom as we suffer life's bumps and bruises. His ability to be cognizant of the starry-eyed beauty of a new relationship while knowing that it is often merely a phase that will eventually be weathered by the realities of our complex selves is a trait to be admired and even coveted by the weary and jaded.

Cibo Matto's Yuka Honda

Brian Wilson's chord progressions tell the most heartbreaking yet beautiful and silently intense story of the duality of life, all from a place of hope. The six-bar intro of "Don't Talk (Put Your Head on My Shoulder)" is worth a thousand books. I consider it to be one of the greatest chord changes ever written.

Deftones' Stephen Carpenter

What I love most about *Pet Sounds* is how much it influenced Mr. Bungle's *California* record. I feel like it's the same album, ultimately—I mean, that's the true California sound right there. I just love Mr. Bungle and how they can go from beauty to straight-bust-your-face-open. I can only imagine what the Beach Boys would have done if they had some really high-gain amps and just crushed you.

Primal Scream's Bobby Gillespie

Screamadelica was greatly influenced by *Pet Sounds*. It's all over that album, in those minor chords, that plaintive sense of melody, and the gentleness as well: the way he used percussion like a soft drum machine. We never had a drummer as good as Hal Blaine from the Wrecking Crew, but we could start sampling shit. After we discovered *Pet Sounds*, along with keyboards and drum loops, our songs became a lot softer.

The Church's Steve Kilbey

It was 1981 and the Church had our first hit single. It was a balmy night and we were staying in a lovely apartment overlooking the Pacific Ocean. We smoked some weed, and our drummer stuck in a cassette tape of *Pet Sounds*, which I had never heard before. Suddenly, the warm night, gentle weed, palm trees, twinkling stars, and the smell of chlorine from the swimming pool all coalesced perfectly with this most divine and delicate music that was pumping off an old-fashioned ghetto blaster. How I marveled at those clever, quasi-classical arrangements and those complex vocal harmonies, the music perfectly suggesting love and summer nights and sweet, sweet romance. Then the most beautiful track, "Let's Go Away for a While," came on—it was the sound of longing and future days.

Tortoise's Jeff Parker

The album is almost futuristic. It sounds like it's from a different world. I aspire to make music as beautifully arranged as that. Even just the instrumental interlude from "I Just Wasn't Made for These Times"— with the Tannerin and a different bassline in a different key going underneath—it's some crazy stuff, like Burt Bacharach on acid.

Washed Out's Ernest Greene

I grew up hearing the big singles from *Pet Sounds* on the oldies station my mom would listen to constantly but I remember the songs feeling a bit different. They were catchy, but there was something peculiar that was just under the surface. I realize now that its peculiarity came from the sheer complexity of the songwriting and arrangement—that there were so many instruments and harmonies present that my young ears weren't used to hearing. I feel like with each listen I'm growing to appreciate it more and more. That is perhaps the biggest compliment I can give *Pet Sounds*—that after so many years of listening, I'm still learning new things from it.✍

RON HART *is a freelance journalist based in New Jersey.*

PITCHFORK PIC

FANS ENJOY THE VIEW AT THE WOODSTOCK MUSIC FESTIVAL

BETHEL, NEW YORK, 15TH-17TH AUGUST 1969